selling
(without selling)
4½ steps to success

Carol Super
with
Ronald D. Gold

AMACOM AMERICAN MANAGEMENT ASSOCIATION
New York ı Atlanta ı Brussels ı Chicago
Mexico City ı San Francisco ı Shanghai
Tokyo ı Toronto ı Washington, D.C.

Special discounts on bulk quantities of AMACOM books are available to corporations, professional associations, and other organizations. For details, contact Special Sales Department, AMACOM, a division of American Management Association, 1601 Broadway, New York, NY 10019. Tel.: 212-903-8316. Fax: 212-903-8083.
Web site: www.amacombooks.org

This publication is designed to provide accurate and authoritative information in regard to the subject matter covered. It is sold with the understanding that the publisher is not engaged in rendering legal, accounting, or other professional service. If legal advice or other expert assistance is required, the services of a competent professional person should be sought.

Library of Congress Cataloging-in-Publication Data

Super, Carol.
    Selling without selling : 4 1/2 steps to success / Carol Super with Ronald D. Gold.— 1st ed.
        p. cm.
    ISBN 0-8144-7186-2
    1. Selling. I. Gold, Ronald D. II. Title.

HF5438.25.S865 2003
658.85—dc21

                                                          2003011347

Various names used by companies and individuals to distinguish themselves or their products can be claimed as trademarks. Such names are used in this book for editorial purposes only, with no intention of trademark violation; that is, such names are not utilized herein to attempt to imply or denote false authorship, sponsorship, or endorsement, nor to create any misleading claim or association as to the source or content of this work. All such names are in initial capital letters. Individuals and companies should be contacted for complete information regarding their trademarks and registration.

Printing number
10 9 8 7 6 5 4 3 2 1

This book is dedicated to the loving memory of Victor Cahn and Bernard Gold, our fathers and lifelong salesmen.

contents

Foreword VII

Preface IX

Acknowledgments XI

Introduction: Why Would *You* Be
Interested in This Book?. 1

STEP 1: ATTITUDE

1   Understanding Responsibility, Mission,
    and *Response*-Ability 7

STEP 2: RAPPORT

2   Building Rapport with Potential Clients. 39

3   Using the Super Theory of *Relate*-tivity 59

STEPS 3 TO 4½: THE PROCESS—INQUIRY, PRESENTATION, AND THE CLOSE

4 Harnessing the Power of Inquiry 87

5 Creating a Successful Presentation 109

6 Recognizing the Close—Just Reconfirm
   and Ask "When" 123

PROSPECTING AND POINTS TO PONDER

7 Overcoming Obstacles to Success 129

8 Prospecting 139

9 Everybody Hates Making Cold Calls 145

10 Learning Super's Secrets of Sales
   Tool Maintenance 159

11 Lagniappe 165

   Index 173

   Author's Bio 178

foreword

SO MUCH OF our success in business and in life depends on our
ability to sell our ideas, our products and services. America wouldn't
be the great economic world power if it were not for the great sales
people who make sales every single day. Think about the book you're
holding in your hands. It was placed in the bookstore because thou-
sands of sales people sold something. In order for this book to exist,
a salesperson had to sell trees to a paper mill. To harvest the trees,
somebody had to sell logging equipment to a logging contractor. In
order to get the logs to the paper mill, somebody had to sell a special
truck to transport the logs to the paper mill. For a paper mill to exist,
it takes an investment of about one billion dollars. Somebody had to
sell the banks on the idea that this would be a good investment that
will ultimately yield high dividends. For a paper mill to be built, it
takes about 12,000 sales calls, 4,000 proposals, 2,400 sales closed, 180
sales canceled and possibly five law suits. After the paper was manu-
factured, somebody had to sell the paper for this book to the printer.
To print this book, somebody had to sell the printer on a multimil-
lion-dollar press. Somebody had to sell a bindery machine. The
printing company would not be in business if it were not for their

sales team calling on publishing houses, writing multipage proposals in order to secure the order for printing this book. After this book got printed it would have gone nowhere without the concentrated efforts of the publisher's sales people making calls on bookstore chains extolling the virtues of *Selling Without Selling.* Yes, nothing happens unless somebody sells something.

Selling is a wonderful profession. Think of some of the sales people who were involved selling the machinery for the paper mill, or the equipment for the printing company. Some of them made enough commission to buy a Corvette or a forty-foot power boat. The selling profession has created many millionaires. Yes, wonderful things can happen when somebody sells something and does it well.

This book is all about selling well. I view selling as one of the best performing arts. The best actors make their art disappear. The same is true with great sales people; they don't focus on selling, because people hate being sold by pushy sales people, but they love buying from great sales people. Great sales people don't sell; they just help people get what they want. Like this book. It will help you get what you want.

Gerhard Gschwandtner
Founder and Publisher
Selling Power magazine

preface

FOR MANY YEARS, my associates, my company management, and even some of my clients have asked me the same question: "Carol, year after year you're tops in your field; your company even awarded you an accolade never given to another salesperson: *Salesperson of the Decade.* Just what is it that makes you so successful so consistently, not just during the good times, but the bad times, too?"

I realized that in order to tell people what the so-called secret is, I'd have to analyze and define it. Was it something I could pass along to others or was it simply unique to me?

You must be thinking, "What could this book possibly offer that would be different from all of the books, seminars, and tapes that I've already listened to, or watched?" Well, I can guarantee you this: When you've completed this book, you'll have a new point of view that will enable you to harness abilities you might not know you possess and to become a significantly more successful salesperson.

It has always been my belief that people are not "sold" anything. They make a decision to buy. Isn't that the same thing? Nope.

I could never be "sold" tickets to a baseball game. Baseball bores me. But, I would certainly be interested in buying tickets to an exciting entertainment event with color, conflict, emotion, and fun—that could be shared with people I like. This book is about creating sales through influencing the buying decision. That is very different from traditional selling, and you are going to discover why.

acknowledgments

THE FOLLOWING people helped to make this book possible. They're not listed in order of the importance of their contributions, as in *Consumer Reports,* but if this book does indeed make you more successful, as it is intended to, they all deserve a great measure of credit.

Ellen R. Kadin is the AMACOM senior acquisitions editor who green-lighted the book. It was her insight and intuition that made it possible for this book to be published. She also guided these "first timers" through the unfamiliar publishing process with great expertise, patience, good humor, and friendship.

We are also amazed at the improvements in the manuscript that took place after it passed through the master hands of Ellen and copyeditor, Mary Miller. The care they took with every word, phrase, and comma has contributed immeasurably to the finished product before you—a vastly improved version of the original manuscript.

In guiding this work to publication, Jim Bessent, associate editor, was the "go-to guy" for every detail. With infinite patience and skill, he made sure that every piece was in place exactly when and how it needed to be. He had to be a diplomat, manager, referee, and confidant—all tasks that he performed with consummate professionalism and warmth.

Computer magician Jake Garver cleverly created our celebrity morphs, and master artist Tom Bruno transformed our rough sketches into printworthy illustrations.

Carol's great-looking cover photo was crafted by skilled lensman Dennis Vechiero.

Brian Azar, the Sales Doctor, is a professional coach whose "you can do it, you should do it" attitude gave us the guts to even attempt this project. Brian, who lives what he preaches, was an inspiration to us and brought us to Ellen.

If Carol had to identify a single mentor, it would be Carl Polsky, a former professor at the Wharton School and close family and personal friend. Carol's mother served as Carl's nanny when she was a young woman. Carl's intelligence, wisdom, and warmth have served as a "rock" through all of life's challenges—personal, professional, and financial. This book is evidence of his support.

Kim Breese, former COO of Dow Jones and lifelong friend, first told Carol that, "You can sell rings around the people I know; why don't you go into sales and let me get you in contact with our human resources person." And that was the beginning of the job search.

Gail Blanke, whose excellent course called Life Designs, helped Carol to focus on her career goals and ultimately decide to become a sales trainer; her compassionate cohorts there were Vivian Ebersman and Lue Ann Eldar.

A salesperson simply cannot be successful without great management. Here are some who have made the biggest difference in Carol's career: Mike Lape, former general sales manager of KYW TV, was willing to see Carol when she was a pure greenhorn, guide her through the labyrinth of the Philadelphia TV market, and later hire her.

Don Heller, former sales manager of WKBS TV, Channel 48, "saw something" and hired Carol for her first sales job, right out of teaching. Bob Schailey, former Media Networks' national sales manager, having seen more than one hundred applicants, had the courage and foresight to hire Carol in spite of her lack of experience in selling print.

John Stephens, now a top manager at 3M Company, demonstrated that warmth, intellect, and quiet self-confidence are qualities that can add up to a spectacular manager.

Allen Dunstan, now a sales manager with Newspapers First, made Carol stretch, promoted her strengths to top management, and taught her how to successfully play the corporate game.

Pat Farrell showed that it is possible to be a strong—as well as a creative—manager, a charming woman, and a supportive colleague simultaneously.

Mark Ford, now president of Times 4 Media, is a pure motivational genius. He has refined and perfected the delicate maneuvering of carrot-and-stick. He is charismatic, energetic, brilliant, focused, and an ideal role model for leadership.

Jamie Pentz, now the associate publisher for Mountain Sports Media, knows what it takes to "make it easy" for salespeople to succeed. Everybody likes and admires Jamie Pentz and that is why people work so hard to succeed for him.

Rob Reif, her current manager, follows in the footsteps of Jamie Pentz and adds the concept of motivating clients through the usually ignored combination of fun and follow-through.

Wayne Powers, president of Media Networks, is unflappable under fire, possesses a titanic work ethic, and inspires tremendous confidence in his troops.

Amanda Kanaga, vice president at Media Networks, is an assertive and very intelligent role model for women at the top, who manages both career and family with aplomb.

Brendan Condon, Vice President of Finance at AOL/TW, is perhaps the most well-rounded "financial guy" on the planet. He proves that it is possible to simultaneously be a talented numbers cruncher, a talented people person, and a hell of a piano player.

It is nearly impossible for any woman to be successful without the caring support of those colleagues who became "girlfriends." In this case, it has been Angela Odorfer, a creative, talented confidante and now a fabulously successful, ever-so-hard-working sales manager, and the one to whom I go with my questions; Midge Winikoff, to whom all are drawn, who is both a riot and empathetic; Barbara McGonnell, who is completely loyal, charming, and the quintessential colleague; and Suzanne Dawson, a sharp, caring, and superbright giver.

Our daughter, Shanti Gold, the Associate Marketing Director of the *New York Daily News,* and who is perfect in every way, donated her expertise toward ensuring that the book flowed well. She sweetened her suggestions with constant praise that helped sustain us through the arduous editing process.

And, of course, our mothers: Carol's mother, Erna Cahn, who constantly and lovingly reminded us "to make this book interesting and one that people will want to read," and Ron's mother, Gwen Gold, who constantly and also lovingly reminded us that if we're writing it, it will be great.

why would *you* be interested in this book?

I once confided to my husband that I was concerned about not being a professional like a doctor or lawyer and that I had a deep-down fear of being a bag lady. He told me something that put me at ease and changed my way of thinking. He said:

Being a great salesperson means that you are a true professional. It also means that you will always be in demand and that you will make a good living. There is always a severe shortage of skilled sales professionals.

YOU'RE A SALESPERSON. Whether you are selling a product or service or you are an executive selling your ideas to management or employees, selling is what you do. It is what we *all* do. But isn't there some aspect of selling that makes you want to stop doing it?

Is it because most of the time you feel battered? Do you feel that your job is an uphill battle filled with hours of pursuit and rejection—toiling to wrest a sale from an immovable force?

Well, maybe it is not quite that dramatic, but, basically, I think that's why you're reading this now. Selling is just so *difficult*.

I am a successful salesperson; however, I don't sell, so I avoid the "pain" of the conventional sales process.

My plan is to change your point of view about your job and how you approach it. I am going to tell you in easy-to-understand, step-by-step detail how it can be done. And, using the information in this book, you're going to be more financially successful at what you do. You are also going to feel better about yourself and your profession.

The 4½ Steps to Success

So, here they are, right up front:

Step 1: Attitude

Step 2: Rapport

Step 3: Inquiry

Step 4: Presentation

Step 4½: Close!

Selling is a process, just not the one most of us are taught. My success process is based on 4½ steps that are very simple to understand

and to execute. However, they *are* synergistic. Together, they are far greater than the sum of the individual steps. If you leave one step out, the synergy is destroyed—and so is its power to create success. If you forget a step, you can go back for it during the process, but you cannot ignore it.

What about the half step, or the close? Although most salespeople may consider it to be the most crucial and difficult to achieve, with my process it is hardly even a step at all. When you follow my first four steps, the close has occurred already. You still have to ask for it, of course, but it is a foregone conclusion.

step 1 : attitude

chapter 1

understanding responsibility, mission, and *response*-ability

THIS IS A BOOK about achieving success by altering your perceptions of your profession, yourself, and other people. It is also a book about the communication process. These new perspectives are the keys to what will soon be your personal framework for success.

From responsibility to *response*-ability, Part 1 will guide you through exciting new ways of looking at what you do everyday. You will begin to harness the power of the *Selling Without Selling* point of view.

Responsibility Toward Others

In the final analysis the one quality that all successful people have is the ability to take on responsibility.

—Michael Korda, author of *Power*

At this point, you might be thinking, "Hold on a second! *You're* going to tell *me* about responsibility? Please! After all, isn't it my strong sense of responsibility that drives me to get out there and push and sell, and push some more?"

I am promising to make you a better salesperson, and yet I am choosing to start by talking about what is, no doubt, already one of your strongest points: a powerful sense of responsibility. My reason is that although a sense of responsibility is one of a salesperson's strongest assets, most people in sales are not using it correctly.

Let's take a quick look at the word *responsibility*. It is derived from the Latin word *respondere*, which means "to reply." The word also means a duty, a charge, or an obligation. That's the definition most often used. However, the *replying* aspect of the word is what will make the big difference in your life.

Even without knowing you, I can tell you what the common threads of your early successes were. I can tell you how you were able to get people to buy what you were selling.

How do I know?

Because at the most basic level people always make decisions based on the belief that they are somehow making their lives better. So if you show them how you can help them accomplish that, they will listen. Even if just pleasing you makes them feel good, that's enough. If, therefore, your attitude really is "I'm here to make your life better; in fact I feel responsible for making your life better," you'll have the key to unlocking a thousand doors.

Perhaps the best salesperson my husband Ron and I ever encountered was a rug merchant in Morocco. Yet, when we first met him, he wouldn't even talk about rugs or answer any of our questions about them, including what prices we were considering paying. Instead, he asked us about our lives and lifestyle. Since he knew that we would definitely want something that would enhance our lives, he asked about our lives in the United States, our daughter, and our home.

In a short time, we came to feel that his objective was not to sell us a rug but to make us aware of how good we would *feel* if this rug were a part of our lives. Price became incidental because, of course, something as fine, unique, and of such great workmanship will be beautiful for many generations. How can you put a price on that? "This is not a rug," he told us, "but rather a wonderful legacy to your children." We soon knew that "acquiring" that rug would improve our lives far beyond what we would be paying for it. So, naturally, we bought it. Your job is to serve . . . not to sell.

"I'M HERE TO HELP YOU"

Eighty percent of success is showing up.

—Woody Allen, comedian, writer, actor, director

My husband and I had been looking for a rug for a long time, and to be honest, had become cynical and defensive. By the time we arrived in Morocco, we truly had heard it all before. Professional buyers, the people you want to sell to, are no different. But no matter who you are meeting with, if they honestly feel you can make their lives better, they are much more likely to welcome what you have to offer.

Let's say that you're representing a state-of-the-art telecommunications system complete with all of the latest high-speed hardware and software bells and whistles. Is it a ridiculous premise to say to them that your system will make their lives better? Isn't it better to discuss the speed, ease of operation, and technical support your company offers?

No, it is not.

The problem is, that approach activates a potential buyer's defense mechanisms and will prompt questions such as, "How much is this going to cost me?" On the other hand, if buyers truly feel that you are there to help them achieve greater professional success, respect, and admiration, they are much more likely to want to listen to you.

So, you must ask yourself what you have to offer that can make this person's life better. You want the person to know that you feel responsible for making his life better. You need to show the person that buying whatever you're selling can, for example, help make her more successful, or even make her company more successful. "Imagine," you might say, "how you are going to feel when your client or your manager realizes what you are proposing. Imagine what people are going to think of you when you show them this concept. People are going to hold you in high regard when they see your recommendation. Because it has been a secret, you will be a hero for your discovery."

But what about those people who already know about your product, let's say a telecommunications system, but don't believe that it could make their lives better? How do you convince them? You do it by finding another way to make them feel that they are speaking to someone who feels responsible for their well-being, rather than someone who is merely trying to sell them something.

We're already at a deeper level than mere sales techniques (to be discussed later), which are, nevertheless, valid and crucial to a sale.

On a superficial level, buyers believe that they are talking to a salesperson, and you might think that you are talking to a potential buyer. But if you can go beyond that level, a transformation occurs where you're seen as a person who has something to offer beyond a car, telecommunications system, magazine space, or a computer.

Well, that's simple. Now you know what you must do to be more successful—just show someone that you feel responsible for their well-being. And that might sound wonderful, but don't put the book away just yet. Merely knowing what to do won't earn you one extra dollar. The rest of this book will show you how to do it.

TO BE BELIEVED, YOU MUST BELIEVE

Believing in your product 100 percent will make you a great salesperson, because you will be real. People can sense fakes, even if it's only 1 percent fake. You must be a solid 100 percent or you will not be successful for very long.

—Donald J. Trump, Chairman and President, The Trump Organization

The next step is to learn how to create this perception of responsibility for making other people's lives better. First, you must believe in yourself and your mission to make your prospect's life better. That is not as easy as it sounds. Your managers have ingrained in you that you're selling a product or a service. You've always worked within a paradigm of selling something. Now you need to change that paradigm.

You can no longer see yourself as a salesperson selling to a buyer. If you believe one game and talk another, you simply won't be believable. And credibility is everything. You really are recreating your own self-image, shifting from thinking of yourself as a salesperson—get that sale, close that customer, etc.—to one of helper, or facilitator.

Doctors certainly don't think of themselves as "pill pushers" or "prescription providers," but rather as people who can bring you good health. A good history teacher isn't merely trying to make students memorize information, but rather to bring history to life and give them an appreciation of their place in it. Architects don't simply design structures; they actually improve the quality of people's lives.

Now, how do you get others—your prospects, your clients—to believe that it is your mission to make their lives better? What are your thoughts when you first meet someone? What do you think that person is thinking about you?

When I speak with someone for the first time, I don't think that the other person is wary of me nor do I go into the meeting visualizing that this will be a confrontational one. If we agree that a person will want what is being offered because it makes his life better, he will have the confidence to believe that the salesperson has the responsibility for doing so.

As a sales professional, I think of myself as a Princess Charming. I carry a sparkling glass slipper that will fit only certain, very special feet. Happily ever after can occur only if the slipper fits the foot. It cannot be jammed on or padded to give the appearance of a good fit. To paraphrase attorney and great philosopher Johnny Cochrane, "If it doesn't fit . . . quit." Although you might need to convince the person to try the slipper on—that is, "it will look so great on you . . . people will be so impressed . . . it's so affordable," etc.— remember, your responsibility is to improve someone's life, not to sell the person a glass slipper that doesn't fit.

"YOU'RE SPECIAL"

One sure way of instilling confidence in a prospect is for you to acknowledge that your product or service is *not good for everyone,* and explain why the person you are speaking to is *part of a select group.* Mention that you have chosen this person because you truly feel this is a perfect match between product and customer. You're certain of this perfect match because of the "success you've had with other similar companies," or because of "an emerging trend" in the person's field, or perhaps "the unique capabilities your product or service could provide to their company." In any case, you must assure potential buyers that you would never waste your time or theirs with a frivolous discussion.

A great salesperson not only truly believes in their product but understands and sincerely takes as much interest in their client's business as in their own.
— Carolyn Forte, Associate Director, Good Housekeeping Institute

Another way to instill confidence is to show your prospects or clients that you've done your homework. For you to convince your prospect that this truly is a perfect match, you need to know what this person "is about" and what her or his company's needs are. One great way to obtain an insight into this information is to go to the client's Web page. Annual reports are another good source of discovering corporate needs. Speaking with company employees, attending trade association meetings, and visiting company branches are other effective ways to analyze and assess needs.

A third way to instill confidence is to mention your length of service as part of the success stories of similar companies or individuals whom you have helped. For example, I say, "In my more than fifteen years of working with Media Networks, we have found that companies that have large ticket items to sell have the best success rate with us. Let me show you what others have done to reach those prospects in the elusive, upscale market, who have the disposable income to afford a product like yours."

And then I name names, such as Verizon, Blue Cross/Blue Shield, Yamaha pianos, and other clients associated with their product category (their competition) and discuss how each has successfully used the medium. And, of course, I show them the advertisements of these companies.

Finally, in my business of selling print ad space, it's a good idea to compliment other media for what they do well. For example, it is helpful to recognize the increase in awareness that broadcast offers, because of its ability to bring sight, sound, and emotion to prospects.

At the same time, however, I also point out the competition's shortcomings. For example, I might mention the zapping of commercials, or the fact that broadcast media can't target a market as well as my company does. In other words: *Respect the competition but not at the expense of your own product.*

Responsibility Toward Yourself

I cannot always control what goes on outside, but [I] can always control what goes on inside.

—Wayne Dyer, leader in the field of self-development; author, *Your Erroneous Zones*

We've talked about your responsibility toward others, now let's look at your responsibility to *yourself* . . . and getting the job done. Meeting this responsibility involves having a positive attitude, knowing your mission, keeping your commitments, focusing on what is important, developing priorities, and setting and meeting standards of professionalism.

ATTITUDE

We are what we think. All that we are arises with our thoughts. With our thoughts we make the world.

—Buddha

I once read that a major business school study concluded that a positive attitude is 93 percent more important to success than information, intelligence, and skill combined. Combined? That's mind-boggling. Clearly, a positive attitude is an absolute necessity in your quest for success.

Knowing the importance of a positive attitude, however, is only the first step in achieving and maintaining it. In business, where ongoing rejection is an unpleasant fact, keeping a positive attitude requires study, practice, and passion.

I always try to focus on the difference between what I can control, what I can't control, and the gray area of influence between them. It's like two overlapping circles (see Figure 1-1). I put the vast majority of my efforts into what I can control. That includes the discipline of making my daily calls, my follow-ups, my preparation, my research,

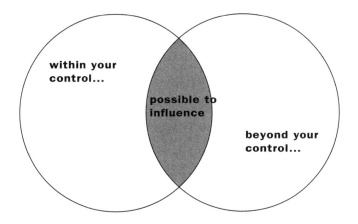

FIGURE 1-1 Focus on what you can control, not what you can't

etc. I try to waste no time whatsoever on what I cannot control. I strive to understand the difference and to simply do the best I can in the gray area.

Let me be very clear. I'm not insinuating that I never become upset by rejections that are beyond my control. I simply don't blame myself! If a rejection is in my control, I take action. I learn from it. I stay focused on my objectives. I stay positive. If it's not in my control, I just use my ready string of expletives and move on.

Oh, God, give us the serenity to accept what cannot be changed, courage to change what should be changed, and wisdom to distinguish the one from the other.
—Reinhold Niebuhr, renowned anti-Nazi theologian

People you are talking to or dealing with can tell instantly when you're feeling down or distracted. They will likely interpret it as a lack of enthusiasm, which means they will believe that you don't care, which will not bode well for you.

Before you interact in business, make certain that your positive attitude index is maxed out. I'm not saying that you should be a phony. Make it real. You have a great deal to feel great about. You're providing an important service. You're a positive part of many lives. You're contributing to the success of others as well as your own. Your opportunities are endless.

I agree with motivational speaker and sales guru Tony Robbins who says you should always physically prepare yourself for success. In a course I once took with him, Robbins exhorted: "Sit up straight. Don't slump. Smile. Look in the mirror that should always be on your desk. Stand up when you're on the telephone. Breathe deeply, from your diaphragm. Sound positive."

YOUR MANTRA OF SELF-AFFIRMATION

Through the years, I have developed a mantra of self-affirmation. It is a list of positive things about my life and me. I recite it to myself when I walk in to work. I close my eyes and recite it to myself when circumstances conspire to bring me down. I use this mantra as a tool to stay focused on the good things in my life so that my attitude can stay positive and that is what I project.

Don't forget until it's too late that the business of life is not business, but living.

—B.C. Forbes

Part of my personal mantra, which I developed at the Silva Mind Control Course, is, "Every day in every way I get better and better. Good things happen to me. Negative thoughts cannot touch me at any level. Every second, every minute of every hour of every day, I am revitalized and restored. I am smart, sophisticated, sensitive, svelte, and successful. The universe works with me. God provides."

It is also very important to have written self-affirmations that you can use daily.

Q: ATTITUDE: WHAT'S LUCK GOT TO DO WITH IT?
A: PLENTY!

Sometimes you do everything right and bomb out. Sometimes you leave town and everything comes zipping through. Sometimes it's luck. We don't understand it. We can't control it. We simply must accept it. Maybe some people really are luckier than others. Who knows?

Here is my opinion on luck: The harder you work, the luckier you get. I don't know who said it first, but I live by it. (It's also the line that my management uses if anyone ever mentions how lucky I seem to be.)

Les jeux sont fait. (Let the chips fall where they may.)

—Jean Paul Sartre, existentialist philosopher

OVERCOMING THE NEGATIVE BELIEF VOICES

We have all had negative beliefs: you, me, Ted Turner, George Bush, Winston Churchill, even Albert Einstein. Conscious or unconscious, we have little voices telling us that we don't have what it takes to be successful. Maybe it was a parent or sibling or teacher constantly chiding you for not doing things right. "No, no, no! Wrong, wrong, wrong! You're never going to get it!"

Maybe it was being taunted by school friends. Maybe it was an employer or boss who put you down in order to feel more important. Those little voices are there, and they're dangerous.

Falling is not in my vocabulary.
—Jean Paul Petite, world famous tightrope walker

I cannot overstress the importance of being aware of these negative belief demons. Don't try to bury them deeper. Face them. Recognize them. Overcome them with your mantra of self-affirmation. They cannot argue with your success.

MOOD TOYS AND RITUALS

It would be great if I could come into work every day, throw a switch, and be 100 percent ready to put into practice all the knowledge I've worked so diligently to accumulate. Unfortunately, it doesn't happen that way. First, I need to switch on my "in-the-mood toys."

I've had my office feng shui-ed (a cubicle can be feng shui-ed too). Feng shui is the ancient Chinese process of placing everything in a space in such a way as to maximize its effectiveness in your life. My desk faces my doorway at a proper angle. I have a small water fountain, aromatherapy candles, and uplifting background music softly playing. There is an area for family photographs. There is another area for awards in my field of work.

We are always complaining that our days are few, and acting as though there would be no end to them.

—Seneca

You may think this office design is going overboard. However, people who come into my office can immediately feel its positive influences and often comment about it. Don't underestimate the value of what in-the-mood props and rituals can do for you. After all, what is more important to how well you function than how you feel?

MISSION

Efforts and courage are not enough without purpose and direction.

—John F. Kennedy, 35th President of the United States

To achieve anything in life, we must first identify what we want and how to get it. Too often, we let outside forces determine what we are going to do. In fact, most people actually spend more time planning their vacations than planning what they want from their lives or careers.

When you go on vacation, first you select where you want to go. There are many choices, such as Disney World, Hawaii, Europe, a safari, a dude ranch, skiing, or going to the beach. Whatever concerns you may have, the number one consideration is that you want to go there. You are consciously choosing what you want and what you enjoy doing. In addition, there are other considerations, such as your time frame, your budget, who you are traveling with, or seasonality.

So, what do you do first? Naturally, the easiest way to begin is by *eliminating the places you don't want to go.*

Then, having decided on the places you would like to go, you get as much information as you can about each one. And the more you think about it, the more obvious it becomes to you which destination would be best for you. So, unless you have an exceptional travel agent, the only way you can have a successful vacation is to spend the time, energy, and effort to make it turn out the way *you* want.

Similarly, for your career to be successful, you must spend time each week thinking about it. What does this career planning "stuff" have to do with getting people to put their trust in you? The answer is very simple: Other people will not believe in you unless you believe in yourself. And you can't truly believe in yourself unless you *understand* yourself and your goals.

YOUR MISSION STATEMENT

In the long run, men hit only what they aim at.
—Henry David Thoreau

You need to ask yourself the following questions: "What is my purpose?" "What is my goal?" or, as we say in the twenty-first century, "What is my mission?"

I have my own mission statement, which I am continually revising, and I work on consciously fitting everything I do into that up-to-date framework. If something doesn't fit within my mission statement, I avoid it.

My statement of purpose will undoubtedly be different from yours. Each of us is unique; therefore, our statements of purpose will be too.

How do you formulate your statement of purpose? First, you need to shut out extraneous, negative experiences and open yourself up to the positive feelings within you. Obviously, you want this statement to resonate within you in the most positive way possible. There are several techniques to help you go into your most positive, open state, such as the self-hypnosis techniques found in courses like Silva Mind Control, Deepak Chopra's book *Timeless Mind/Ageless*

Body, and Herbert Benson's *The Relaxation Response.* But I have my own way of doing it.

GO TO YOUR OWN SPECIAL PLACE

Whenever we engage in work that we really love to do, we will always lose track of time and feel an abundance of energy.
—Gerhard Gschwandtner, Publisher, *Selling Power*

When I want to find out what I really want or how to get what I want from others, I use a simple combination of the following relaxation and visualization techniques. They bring you to your most relaxed state of mind—a place where you are completely open and in control of your thoughts.

Begin by sitting back in your chair, arms relaxed, feet flat on the floor, one hand on each leg. Breathe in slowly through your nose and exhale out through your mouth. Now close your eyes. You should be very relaxed. Visualize the number ten in your mind's eye. See every line of the number one and every curve of the number zero. Now visualize number nine . . . number eight. You are going deeper and deeper. You are becoming very relaxed. Now visualize the number seven in all its aspects: the horizontal line, the line slanting down . . . now number six . . . number five. You are becoming even more relaxed . . . four, three, . . . deeper, deeper . . . now two . . . now one. . . . You are now in a relaxed state of mind.

Keep your eyes closed and your body relaxed. Relax your scalp, your eye muscles, while letting go of all the tension in your ears, your nose, and your mouth. Your jaw is relaxed, no longer clenching. Your neck muscles are very relaxed. You can now release the tension in your shoulders, in your arms, in your hands, and all the way through to your fingertips.

Your chest is relaxing; the tension is leaving your entire upper body. Now release the tension in your stomach, your groin, your thighs, and your legs. Your calves are relaxed; you are letting go of all the tension in your feet, down to your toes. Your body is completely relaxed.

Now, you're going to go to a very personal place that is yours and yours alone. It's the most relaxing, peaceful place in your life. Maybe it's a favorite beach, or a stream in the woods, or a special chair. Count from one to three, again visualizing the numbers in your mind's eye. At three, you will go to your special place.

Ready. One . . . *relax*, two . . . *relax*, three . . . you're there. Isn't it wonderful, this special place? Now you're ready to visualize. Staying totally relaxed in your special place, slowly open your eyes.

Now, think about the *good* things the following people would say about you, starting with your:

- Mother

- Best friend

- Father

- Manager

- Spouse

- Peers

- Children

- Best customer or client

Oh wad some power the giftie gie us, to see oursel's as others see us!
—Robert Burns

Now picture yourself many years from now looking down (hopefully) and hearing your eulogy being delivered. Think about what you would like to hear being said about your accomplishments, your contributions, et cetera.

Now, staying completely relaxed in your special place, come back to the present, glowing with the full knowledge of all the positive things said about you. Write a succinct sentence or short paragraph about what you feel your purpose in life should be, both personally and for your career.

Don't worry about "getting it right." There is no "correct" purpose. This can be an ongoing process in which you evaluate, change, add to, and refine what you are saying or writing today.

Just to give you an idea, my own personal statement—at the moment, at least—is "to make the world a better place and to do my best to live every moment to the fullest so that I can enjoy the process of life."

You need to have both a personal and a business mission statement because until you fully develop what you want to achieve as an individual and set your personal goals, you have no platform from which to formulate a vision for your business life. My work statement is "to provide systems that help the business community of New York City achieve greater productivity and an easier life."

Try to write out a mission statement that will inspire you. In the statement, your personal and business goals should mesh. To be effective, these goals must never in any way contradict each other. In case you need additional inspiration, here are what some companies have created for their mission statements:

☛ "[To be] . . . the most innovative enterprise . . . and the preferred supplier in the markets we serve . . . growing through flexible, self-reliant businesses . . . that draw on powerful, evolving core technologies and supply expertise."—The 3M Company.

☞ "To be the leader of, and passionate advocate for, results-driven local market advertising."—Media Networks, Inc./ AOL Time Warner (the company I work for).

☞ "To be regarded as the quality and market leader of the hotel industry worldwide. We are responsible for creating exceptional, profitable results with the investments entrusted to us by efficiently satisfying customers."—The Ritz-Carlton.

☞ "One minor invention every ten days, a major invention every six months."—Thomas Edison, inventor of the phonograph, incandescent light bulb, and much more.

You've already accomplished a great deal in your special place. You can and should return there, at least once every day. But now it's time to return to the real world. Close your eyes. Slowly count from one to three, visualizing each number. When you come to the number three, open your eyes. You should feel refreshed, happy, and have a sense of well-being. One, two, three . . .

What is particularly wonderful about this special place is that you can go there whenever you need relaxation or inspiration, and it doesn't cost a cent! For example, this is what I do when I need to make an especially difficult telephone call, either because I feel the person is intimidating or because the person will be less than pleased to hear from me because of a problem that needs resolution. I take a short trip to my special place and visualize how I want the conversation to unfold. And, guess what? It usually becomes a positive, self-fulfilling prophecy.

Now that you have your first draft of your mission statement, immediately begin to use it. I keep my mission statement in front of my daily planner, so it is the first thing I see when I begin my day. It reminds me of what is important and in what direction I should be heading. It is somewhat like checking your compass when you hike in an unknown area. Your mission statement is true north: so you should check it continually so that you can make any necessary course corrections.

At the end of each week, I evaluate my accomplishments for that week in the context of my mission statement, then I set my goals for the following week within the same context. From your own overall mission statement, you can then ensure that your goals for your role as a businessperson are congruent with your general principles or philosophy.

You may want to work on this continually for the next six months to a year, thinking and refining exactly what it is that is your mission. If you keep your mission and your goals as a successful salesperson in the forefront of your daily thinking and your weekly evaluation of your actions, you will set yourself apart from those who randomly walk through life.

There are definite advantages to knowing your goal or mission. One of these advantages is having the tools needed to prioritize what is important day-to-day, and week-to-week. Do you spend an inordinate amount of time performing unimportant tasks that have nothing to do with your mission or doing work that you could easily delegate to others? Having a mission statement, and keeping it in mind, will go a long way to helping you avoid wasted effort.

It also provides you with a touchstone when you feel that you're drifting. It is a constant reminder of what you are striving to accomplish. It adds to your feelings of self-assurance because you know who you are and where you are going.

VISUALIZATION

The mission statement exercise we have just completed includes one example of the technique of visualization to help make good things happen. There are many other applications as well.

For example, professional athletes like Tiger Woods use visualization to "see" in their minds, and therefore facilitate a positive outcome. Tiger sees the ball going to the hole, and this helps his body do the things it has been trained to do to make that happen.

Businesspeople utilize visualization to see themselves succeeding at important meetings, at tough presentations, and at deal closings. Visualizing their success helps them smoothly do the things they have been trained to do in order to achieve that success.

A successful shot is 50 percent visualization, 40 percent setup, and only 10 percent swing.
—Jack Nicklaus

So, in addition to helping you determine your mission, the visualization process of having a special place that you've just learned provides you with an invaluable method for accomplishing tasks that are important but difficult for you. I've already mentioned how I use it to help me make difficult telephone calls. But I also use it to help me do less-than-favorite chores.

Of my two least-favorite chores, the first is cleaning off the top of my desk. But when I use my relaxation and visualization techniques to see myself clearing off each quadrant of my desk, anxiety and dread are replaced by feelings of accomplishment and pride. My second least-favorite chore is doing my expense account. So, instead of thinking of all the work that needs to be organized, I utilize the visualization and meditation process. I can then see the end result and feel how wonderful it is to be getting back all the money to which I am entitled.

What are some of the things you fear or dread? What tasks cause you serious bouts of procrastination? How do you deal with them? Visualization will help you. Since my early days in television sales in Philadelphia, this visualization technique has been invaluable in helping me to channel my type A energy toward achieving specific goals. It's also helped me to remain calm in very high-pressure situations. In fact, I discovered the importance of relaxation techniques through studying the habits of successful people.

COMMITMENT

Until one is committed, there is hesitancy, the chance to draw back, always ineffectiveness. Concerning all acts of initiative and creation, there is one elementary truth—the ignorance of which kills countless ideas and splendid plans: that the moment one definitely commits oneself, the Providence moves too.

—W. H. Murr, Scottish explorer

Being committed to what you do is another essential factor in being successful. Even when I first began my career in sales—after a stint as a teacher—I was committed to being a professional salesperson. I was determined to learn everything I could about sales and successful selling techniques. Even now, I make time every day to read a professional sales magazine such as *Selling Power,* listen to an audiotape, or read a business-oriented book on selling. In addition, I read the business section of the *New York Times* and parts of the *Wall*

Street Journal. On the weekends, I read *Newsweek* and *Time,* plus business magazines such as *Business Week, Fortune,* and *Forbes.* This commitment to professionalism is essential for success in any field. What do you do on an ongoing basis to upgrade your skills to make you a more effective professional in your field?

Commitment means keeping your word with yourself—not being distracted by the siren song of doing things the easy way or by the distractions that others may put in your path. Almost all successes of major significance were achieved because someone remained committed to a goal. Edison failed hundreds of times before he produced a practical light bulb. Galileo refused to be deterred by circumstance, derision, or doubt. Churchill steadfastly stayed focused in spite of temptations, disapproval, and fears . . . and rallied his countrymen in World War II.

You simply cannot succeed without a fierce sense of commitment. That doesn't mean that you can't have fun or relaxation or enjoyment; just don't let anything lull you away from your awareness of what you promised yourself. For example, I limit personal telephone calls during business hours. I don't play on the Internet at work. I save personal tasks (like shopping) for off-hours.

You will be amazed at how much more you can achieve by keeping a strong awareness of your commitments. Your goals will be achieved much more easily if you keep them alive and a part of everything you do.

FOCUS
The best horse cannot wear two saddles.

—Chinese proverb

Now that you know what visualization or imaging can do for you, it is important to learn how to focus your energies. Knowing what you want and actually concentrating on achieving it are not the same thing. A strong focus is the key to your becoming a successful persuader. Keeping your mission statement in front of you, for example, helps you to focus on fulfilling your mission.

Maybe you are like me and become easily distracted. When I was a student at the Wharton Evening School (which I attended after I left teaching), one of my professors once said to me, "Carol, focus will channel all that wonderful energy, enthusiasm, and excitement you have into a profitable and successful career."

I never forgot those words. Even now, whenever I'm with a client, no matter how much I'd rather talk about our mutual interests, I always remember why I'm in front of this client, what my responsibility is, and what my focus should be. I also have to remind myself to let the client talk instead of talking too much myself.

Learning to visualize is as easy as wanting to do it. When you're taking a photograph, it is not enough to compose and frame the subject matter. There is another step you must take before you press the shutter—you must sharpen the focus. It's the same with non-photographic visualization. For example, it's not enough to visualize making a cold call—you need to clearly picture the way it is going to progress and the successful outcome. In other words, you must focus and visualize to the point where you can actually experience the positive feelings you'll have upon the successful completion of the call.

Most salespeople enjoy constant change, new challenges, and quickly going on to something else—the next sale, the next proposal, or the next meeting. Although this can be a positive trait, it can also make it more difficult to retain one's focus. It is essential to balance unbridled exuberance with concentration and awareness of your mission and goals. Learning to stay on point is one of the most challenging and rewarding steppingstones to success.

INSPIRATIONAL PROPS

I keep photographs around me of things that inspire me to reach my goals, such as places I want to visit, clothing and jewelry I would like to buy, my family and my home. I also display my sales awards and trophies. They are all constant reminders of what working is all about.

Fürst die arbeit, dass denn vergnügen. (First the work, then the pleasure.)

—Erna Cahn, philosopher and my Mom

PRIORITIZATION

There are those who work all day; those who dream all day; and those who spend an hour dreaming before setting to work to fulfill those dreams. Go into the third category because there's virtually no competition.

—Steve Ross, founder of Time Warner

In addition to bringing your visualization into focus, it is important to put your priorities in order, as well. How do you order your priorities? First, you must determine which ones are the most important tasks and focus on them.

Typically, when a painter crafts an image, for example, he or she begins by establishing the major elements of the work. The perspective, the basic palette, the horizon, and the most prominent features must be firmly in place before any detailing can begin.

Obviously, if a painter attempted to portray details first, the finished work—if it could be finished—would be visually chaotic . . . and unsuccessful.

You may want to view the planning of your daily goals as a blank canvas. Define your major elements first, and get into "detailing" only after they are addressed. Your painting will be a successful reflection of your task management skill.

Successful prioritization begins with looking at your client base and asking yourself whether you've done all you can to keep their business—and maximize business from them—before you go after new prospects. It is vital that you remember the 80/20 rule: 80 percent of your business generally comes from 20 percent of your clients. So, you must keep those in the 20 percent group in the forefront of your business day. I have found that losing a client from my base of business means working at least five times as hard to replace the business.

You must also bear in mind that what is most important can change on an hourly basis, and you must be able to adjust your priorities. Basically, this simply means keeping your eye on the ball. The following example shows how I refocus my priorities:

When the deadline for meeting my sales goals is not a major consideration, I seek out the most perfect prospects—those who have big budgets, those who could benefit the most, those from whom I sense the least resistance, and so on. But when deadlines are only days away and I'm still short of my goal, I shift my priorities toward those prospects whom I know have a previously prepared advertisement, whom I may have spoken to before, or who might be open to an incentive.

It is actually very simple: There is a finite amount of time, therefore, if you use up too much of your time on less essential matters, the important tasks will go undone. It's common sense. So, maintain your focus and constantly touch base with your mission statement.

PROFESSIONALISM

I don't believe in circumstances. The people that get on in this world are the people who get up and look for the circumstances they want, and, if they can't find them, make them.
—George Bernard Shaw

Far too many salespeople confuse the term *occupation* with *profession*. The word occupation is simply an identification of what you do, whereas being a *professional* means that you are continually studying your craft, learning and perfecting what you do. It means setting the highest possible standards of ethics and performance and constantly striving to meet those standards. If you perform in a professional manner, you'll find that you are treated with the same respect that professionals earn.

I believe that great salespeople are made, not born. Let's face it, in any profession, some are blessed with greater natural talent than others. Baseball champions such as Hank Aaron and Joe DiMaggio worked hard to bring this talent to its peak. But Pete Rose was given less of it to begin with, so he had to work even harder. The results of his intensity of purpose are legendary. Whether you're a DiMaggio or a Rose, only by putting the necessary effort into your professional performance can you become a star.

Response-Ability

Nothing showed me more clearly how difficult it is to get others to listen to you than my first job, which was teaching history to high school kids. Before I began teaching, I thought it would be like the movie *Field of Dreams*. You know, "Build it and they will come."

Here I was, a well-educated person who even found time to read *The Wall Street Journal*—with the laudable goal of teaching these young people about our past. I was in for a shock. Not only did they not care that I read *The Wall Street Journal* or that I had wonderful information to impart, but they also had absolutely no interest in the subject or even in being in a classroom. What was I going to do?

After all, it was up to me to enlighten them about the past and its influence on today. Nothing in my psyche was more important than showing them the wonder of the events that happened before they were born and the impact the past had on their lives today.

I had a mission to accomplish, which was making the lives of my students better. And it looked like *Mission Impossible*.

I gained new appreciation for the wisdom of poet William Butler Yeats, who once said, "Education is not filling a bucket but lighting a fire." I realized that before I could light their fire and get them to respond favorably to what I was offering (or selling), I first had to respond to them. That is, my success would depend on my *response-ability*, or my ability to respond.

In order to enhance my ability to respond to them and, therefore, the likelihood of their responding to me, I first had to learn who they were and what was important to them—from their home life to their social life. Once I had this information, it became a simple matter to harness my skills to present things from their perspective.

For example, because I knew that most of my students were from blue-collar families, I invited them to literally act out the formation of labor unions from the working person's perspective. The kids who fantasized about being leaders were selected to be part of the Samuel Gompers group—the union organizers. The tough kids wanted to be the Pinkerton guards—the private police officers hired by companies to keep unions out. The kids who tended to speak out of turn were made corporate executives. And, as a concession to their raging hormones, the factory where they worked made screws. The burst of activity caused by "lighting the fire instead of filling the bucket" caused some raised eyebrows at the school—until it became clear that is was immensely successful.

They soon realized that the information I was offering was not only valuable but would actually benefit them. They weren't "buying" the history stuff to please me. They discovered that I was offering it to them to enrich their lives.

In other words, I had to help them make a paradigm shift; I had to let them know that I was their servant and that I was offering them something, which, from their perspective, was wonderful. Of course, this meant that I needed to be well versed on their perspective.

When you care enough about the person to whom you are presenting to learn how to respond to them on *their terms*, it predisposes them to take you seriously and to open up to what you are proposing. By responding to another person instead of pushing your ideas on them, you're far more likely to have them on your side—and eager to work with you rather than against you.

> When my husband and I began our search for a new home, we discarded an experienced, well-regarded real estate person who seemed to have little interest in us for a novice who showed a lot of interest even though she had no developed skills.
>
> For no reason we can fathom, the experienced person decided instantly that we were not serious buyers. This was not based on any information she received from us, because she asked us for virtually no information. She seemed to expect *us* to follow up with *her*.
>
> The novice, on the other hand, though green in the business, had good basic instincts. She made up for her lack of polish with what we felt was a sincere effort to make us happy. She showed us homes at various locations, of various sizes, at many prices, until she (finally) got a good sense of just who we were and what we were looking for.
>
> She stayed with us. She stayed in touch. She let us know that finding a perfect match for us was her prime focus. We were

> made to feel, whether true or not, that we were her most important clients.
>
> In the end, it was she who brought us to our dream house. She made us happy. She made a fat commission. The experienced person made nothing.

Using your understanding of other people's buying proclivities is a powerful but gentle persuasive tool. It is manipulation in one of its most effective and positive forms. Because the prospect sincerely feels that the buying decision is his or hers, the prospect will do more to make it happen and will look to you for support in that decision by asking for research, competitive information, price adjustments, et cetera.

It's very simple: The better you understand someone, the more effectively you can communicate with that person. *The more effectively you communicate, the more successful you'll be.*

Statesman, author, and artist Sir Winston Churchill was one of history's great masters of the English language. In spite of having to overcome speech difficulties, his words gave the English people the courage and resolve they needed to survive and ultimately prevail in World War II. He had the entire language at his ready disposal, yet he chose simple words that were often presented in a nearly poetic cadence.

On June 4, 1940, after the disastrous retreat from Dunkirk, France, he spoke the following few words, which rallied a nation and remain to this day a prime example of the immense power of the spoken word: "We shall fight on the beaches, we shall fight on the landing grounds, we shall fight in the fields and in the streets, we shall fight in the hills; we shall never surrender."

He knew and understood his audience. He was born of nobility, but he communicated magnificently with the general public because he spoke to them in a manner he knew they could relate to.

Remember Sir Winston. Know your audience. Care about your audience. Relate to your audience.

You are now armed with your mission statement, which has your personal and business goals. You have your focus and your sense of commitment. You have developed a responsibility to yourself and understand the importance of *response*-ability. You have created a foundation upon which to build relationships with others. You are now ready to proceed to Step 2 of *Selling Without Selling's* 4½ Steps to Success, which is how to effectively *relate* to others.

step 2 : rapport

building rapport with potential clients

Relating

When I was a young man, I sold vacuums door to door. I had ten seconds to say something important or the door would slam in my face. If the lady of the house kept the door open, I then had fifty seconds to talk to her in a simple, understandable language. I also learned that when she opened the door, I had to look professional. If I wore my leather jacket, she might have thought I was a hoodlum. In addition, I was told never to sell vacuums in a neighborhood that doesn't have carpets. Finally, I discovered that you have to sell yourself first to believe in your product and then you will sell the product to others. Cynical people are not good salespeople.

—Jerry Della Femina, CEO, Della Femina, Rothschild, Jeary and Partners

As a salesperson, I know that you are raring to get your message out and to impress potential buyers with information and numbers. You want to sweep them off their desk chairs and into your commission column. However, it is vital that you control this impulse. Remember, you're not dealing with a role-playing character in a sales-training course. The individual across from you has a personal point of view: a family, a religion, hobbies, and individual preferences.

In order to even begin to relate to that person, you must take some time to build rapport. It's not difficult. Socially, you do it all the time. Show a sincere interest in the person's lifestyle, where and how the person lives, his or her hobbies—even the person's commute to work. Remember what the person says and apply it to everything that occurs in your interactions with her. It very well could be the difference between whether or not a buying decision is made in your favor.

I was once with one of our new salespeople (I'll call him Hank) who had recently moved to New York from out of state and was now living in a suburb of New York City. The media buyer we were with was a confirmed Manhattanite. During our introductory chat with the buyer, Hank blurted out the age-old out-of-towner question: "How do people stand living in this city?" This, of course, was an immediate turnoff to the buyer, which resulted in no sale.

I have also been on calls where salespeople have exhibited profound chauvinistic tendencies, homophobic tendencies, et cetera.

Tina, a salesperson who liked tennis, was in the office of a buyer whose choice of décor demonstrated an obvious love of golf. Incredibly, Tina expressed her disdain for the game of golf, saying that the game was too slow, not enough exercise, and a good walk spoiled. Again, there was no sale.

Tina could have expressed herself in terms of her own lack of patience, skill, and proper attitude necessary to enjoy the game. This would have put the buyer's taste in a positive light and still allowed Tina to express her individuality. Better yet, she could have simply listened more.

The greatest motivational act one person can do for another is to listen.
—Roy B. Moody

There is a rule of thumb I like to use called the 4-to-1 Rule. Here it is. Read, repeat, and remember it:

Your prospect should speak four times more than you do.

You should speak four times less than your prospect.

When you're talking, you're not learning.

Tip: Everyone's favorite topic is himself or herself. People enjoy talking about themselves; and if they're enjoying themselves, they'll be more receptive. I actually landed my first job out of teaching by instinctively translating my nervousness into a focus on the interviewer. He thought I was brilliant—and told me so. I replied that I really hadn't said much, and he said, "I guess that's why you're brilliant."

If you gloss over the rapport-building stage in your initial meeting with the prospect, you'll be ignoring one of your most important tools. Once again, take time and effort to build rapport. It will set you apart. You'll be amazed how well this sincere investment can pay off.

When you ask what are the qualities of a good salesperson, immediately, a picture comes to mind of who that individual might be. She stands out. She is a rare and stoic bird amidst the lionous, competitive world of financial institution data exchange. I use the term bird *because she is graceful, tenacious, knows where she's headed and clearly sees her clients' goals from a bird's-eye view. And when dealing with her, you never feel as if her goals are different from yours. She stays on course with a willingness to shift should inclement conditions surface. She then gets you back on track with everyone arriving at the appropriate desti- nation. She listens attentively, not automatically. She works within your budget constraints and strategic directions; she is resourceful, never for- gets her social graces (birthdays, special events, promotions, etc.). And guess what? You never feel as if you're being "sold up the creek." In fact, you want to send more business her way at any opportunity.*

—Lue Ann Eldar, CEO, Calista Maria,
a not-for-profit agency in the Bronx

Observing

You can observe a lot by watching.

—Yogi Berra, Baseball Hall of Fame catcher and manager

Now that you know how to identify opportunities to relate and have started to understand the prospect's thinking process, it is time to begin using your knowledge to fulfill your responsibility. You want to be someone they feel comfortable with because they will be more likely to trust you and, therefore, buy from you. One of the quickest and easiest ways to begin is by simple observation.

When you first meet your prospect, look carefully at how the person is dressed. If it's a man, is he wearing a special tie? Is the prospect's collar open or closed? Is this person a conservative or a trendy dresser? Where would this person be more comfortable, in Eddie Bauer or Brooks Brothers? If you're meeting a woman, look at her jewelry. Is she wearing something unique? Is she more conservatively dressed, or would you say she's high-fashion?

Look at the person's office environment. Are there photographs of the family? Are there plaques on the wall? What type of artwork is displayed? What type of desk does the person have? How are the chairs arranged? One surefire method of identifying a "control" person, for example, is a seating arrangement that forces you to look up to that person.

You should ask questions and/or make comments about what you have observed. For example, if you see a house in a photograph in the prospect's office, ask about it or compliment it—but only if you mean it. The same advice applies to family photographs, golf memorabilia, the watch the prospect is wearing, and so on. The answers will help you find out more about the person and will comfortably draw the prospect into conversation. If you cannot find anything worth asking about after observing the prospect's office, you can always use the weather or a major news story.

The greatest salespeople I have known pick up their share of the work. They've worked hard to understand my products and my competitors and where their vehicle fits. They don't just bring a media kit; they bring creative opportunities that help me sell my product efficiently and effectively. When I meet with a great salesperson, they never waste my time; they use that time for both my benefit and theirs.

—William J. McCarron, Vice President, Verizon Communications

You're trying to establish common ground to make the buyer feel comfortable around you. My previous company training taught me to come in and immediately begin the "selling Q & A." I found that all this does is put the prospect on guard, whereas, the techniques we've discussed so far will put the person at ease and on your side.

Establishing *common ground* is the beginning of the sales process.

Tip: Try bringing a token gift with you on a first call to use as an ice-breaker. This could be something that represents your company and is useful. I try to integrate this gift when I discuss my company. For example, when I represented 3M Company, I would bring new prospects their own Post-it Note® holder, which could remain on their desks.

What would be appropriate and affordable for you to bring on your first call? If your appointment is late in the afternoon, it's fun and memorable to show up with an interesting low-fat snack to break the ice. When setting the appointment, I also ask whether the prospect prefers coffee or tea, and I bring it along. In this way, I can be more assured that the person will be refreshed and alert.

Mirroring—How It Makes You Look Good

An amazingly easy and effective way to put people at ease and to make them feel that "you're their kind of people" is through mirroring. The process of mirroring is simply noticing the mannerisms of the person to whom you are talking and mimicking them. If the person crosses his or her legs, you cross your legs. If the person leans forward, you lean forward. If the person puts a hand under his or her chin, you put your hand under your chin.

The ingredients that mix to make one salesperson who outshines all others include: A sense of fair play. Accuracy and accountability. Flexibility. A sharp memory. And, they know me and know my clients.

—Paul Benjou, Director of Client Services, Mediaplex, Inc./Adware, Inc.

If the person's speech is slow, speak slowly. If the person's tone is soft, be soft. If the person speaks in clipped sentences, make sure you do so as well. If the person speaks in a high-pitched voice and yours is normally low, raise yours. If the person is wearing glasses and you have glasses, wear them. If not, don't, unless you absolutely need to. Notice the person's simple habits, such as how he or she holds a pen or pencil, any unique gestures, or how the person folds his or her hands.

Don't worry that you will be caught mirroring, because it doesn't happen. If you are not looking for it, you won't see it. It's as simple as that. The more you do it, the more you will see how true this is. If you are nervous about it, begin with your family and friends and see if they notice that you are mirroring. They won't.

Tip: An added bonus of mirroring is that it will help you feel comfortable as well. Many salespeople worry about how they are coming across to their prospects. Mirroring eliminates this worry. Because you are reflecting the other person, you can relax with the knowledge that he or she is comfortable with how you look and with your mannerisms. This method is so easy and foolproof that I sometimes almost feel like it's cheating. But it's not, so use it!

When I first arrived in New York City, I had been single for more than ten years. One of my goals was to meet my soul mate and get married. I read a book called *How to Make a Man Fall in Love with You,* by Tracy Cabot, Ph.D., which discussed the mirroring technique as an excellent way to put your special man at ease.

When I met my future husband, and co-author of this book, at a party in Greenwich Village, I figured that this was a good time to put mirroring to the test. During our first few dates, I made a conscious effort to sit forward when he sat forward, stroke my chin when he stroked his, and lean in when he leaned in. It felt very strange at first, but he didn't seem to be aware of my "game." We were married sixteen months later.

I admit that other factors were at play besides mirroring, but it certainly wasn't my cooking that put him at ease during our early days. It wasn't until we started to write this chapter of our book that he found out that he had been mirrored. (Of course, there's a lot more he still doesn't know.)

Visualizer, Auditory, or Kinesthetic?

One extension of the mirroring process is sensory recognition. Most people have one predominant sensory element: sight, hearing, touch, smell, or taste.

The overwhelming majority of people, roughly 85 percent, process information visually, according to Brian Azar, the Sales Doctor. About 10 percent process information better with their sense of hearing, and the remaining 5 percent are primarily kinesthetic, or "feelers."

There are some simple ways to identify which sense predominates in a person. One surefire tip-off is the way the person uses words or phrases. If a person says things like, "I see our company utilizing your product"; "I *picture* myself one day owning a Lexus"; and "It *looks like* we're going to do business," that person is probably a visualizer. They'd like you to *paint a picture* for them as you describe the benefits, features, and advantages of your product or services. When speaking to these people, I use phrases such as, "I think you'll like the *look* of this"; "Just *look* at these numbers"; and "Wait till you *see* this."

To recognize people who are predominately auditory, "listen" for phrases such as, "I *hear* you"; "It *sounds* good to me"; and "We've got our *ear to the ground*." Be sure that you present information to them in an auditory format, such as, "I think you'll like the *sound* of this plan"; "Just *listen* to these numbers"; and "Wait till you *hear* this."

A great salesperson first and foremost must be a good listener—it's a skill critical to understanding what motivates a client. Secondly, the salesperson must be able to cut to the bottom line and identify what the client really needs. Thirdly, he/she has to communicate effectively and enthusiastically how they will deliver the results the client seeks. And, of course, flexing some creative muscle never hurts, particularly in a service-oriented business.

—Howard J. Rubenstein, President,
Rubenstein Associates Inc.

If you "feel" the person is neither primarily visual nor auditory, then you may assume that he or she is kinesthetic. Remember this term will apply to only 5 percent or so of the population. The kinesthetic person uses phrases such as, "I *feel* this will work well"; "I *sense* the direction in which you are heading"; "I want things to go as *smoothly* as possible"; or "We're in for some *rough* sledding." To really "touch" these people, I use phrases such as, "I understand how you *feel*"; "Get *a handle* on these numbers"; and "You seem to have a good *grasp* of the concept."

In the following exercise, there is a list of phrases that people often use. In the right-hand column, write down whether that phrase identifies a visualizer (V), an auditory (A), or a kinesthetic (K) type of person.

PHRASE	TYPE
1. It's like fingernails on a blackboard.	A
2. Clear as a bell.	A
3. Crystal clear.	V
4. Tied up in knots.	
5. Smooth as silk.	
6. Like a lead balloon.	
7. A home run.	
8. Pretty as a picture.	
9. A slap in the face.	
10. What you're saying is.	
11. You're not listening to me.	
12. It's beautiful.	
13. This does not ring true to me.	
14. Let me show you how it's done.	
15. You're in style.	
16. Let's hear that again.	
17. What wonderful shape this is in.	
18. This makes me nervous.	

PHRASE	TYPE
19. Make the numbers sing.	
20. What am I hearing here?	
21. This is like a bolt out of the blue.	
22. It's a slam dunk.	
23. Repeat that please.	
24. What a pain.	
25. That's a reach.	
26. I'm not comfortable with that.	
27. I see problems.	
28. That's sending a bad signal.	
29. More often we hear . . .	
30. More often we see . . .	
31. More often we feel . . .	
32. Seeing is believing.	
33. Put that in writing.	

The answers are:
1A, 2A, 3V, 4K, 5K, 6V, 7V, 8V, 9K, 10A, 11A, 12V, 13A, 14V, 15V, 16A, 17V, 18K, 19A, 20A, 21V, 22V, 23A, 24K, 25K, 26K, 27V, 28A, 29A, 30V, 31K, 32V, 33V

Another simple way to visually identify whether a person is a visualizer, an auditory, or a kinesthetic type is by the way the person uses his or her eyes when trying to remember.

Try this test on yourself: What was the name of your third-grade teacher? Look for the following: If your eyes moved *upward* and to your left or right, you are probably a Visualizer or at least in a visualizing mood. Here's what a visualizer looks like to another person:

Eyes Up to Your Right   **Eyes Up to Your Left**
(Remembering the past)   (Thinking of the future)

If your eyes went to either side (toward the ears), it's a sign that you're in an *auditory* mode. Here's what an auditory looks like:

Eyes to the Side

Finally, if your eyes moved *downward,* you're probably a kinesthetic.

Eyes Down

It's fun to practice the identification process. You'll be amazed how accurate it is. Just ask anyone you know (or *think you know*) a simple remembering question, such as, "What did you have for lunch yesterday?" Observe the person's eye movement. Make your diagnosis and check it with your subject. Remember, you may be dealing with a kinesthetic who is in an auditory or visual mode. In this case, it's best to deal with that person in the mood they are currently in.

In addition to using the key phrases we discussed, think about how you would give the various types what they want in your presentations to them. The visualizers more than likely want face-to-face meetings, want their presentations peppered with images that they can see and think about in visual terms, and, as we said, want you to paint them a picture. Make reports or charts look visually appealing. They may *look* for results, *envision* a project, *show* others their ideas, and/or want to *see* a written analysis.

Because the auditories are listeners, it's a good idea to include stories or musical references in your presentations. Auditories like to communicate via the telephone or in person and not through memos or letters. Be sure to *listen* well to auditories, who also like to *hear* the sound of their voice. They want to *hear* what you can do for them. Take your time; pay attention to *sounding* good and delivering an organized presentation.

A great salesperson has the passion for the product and the knowledge to convey that passion.
—Laurence J. Kirshbaum, Chairman & CEO, AOL/Time Warner Book Group

The kinesthetics are the sensitive individuals who want you to show them that you care. Find out what is important to them, both personally and professionally. They will usually be open about their feelings. Draw them out; ask them about their values, their families, their positions, and so on. They will willingly accede. When you have lunch or dinner with a kinesthetic, it is good business to sit next to them, rather than across from them, which looks more adversarial.

Kinesthetics are the slowest talkers of the three neuro-linguistic types. They are also slow in making decisions. When speaking to a kinesthetic, you can't be fast-talking or speak too directly to the point. If you do, you'll scare the person off. A kinesthetic responds favorably to a hands-on demonstration. You need to make the person *feel something.*

All these are simple, but effective, mechanisms for relating to other people and being in their world. The more people feel that you are like them, the more relaxed, open, and less defensive they will be. You will also be more at ease knowing that you're making the prospect more comfortable. For example, if you're with a person who demonstrates, by word or décor, an interest in sailing, don't skim over it. Respond. They love sailing. Get that person talking about the boat, his or her trips, how great life is with "just you and the wind." If you don't sail, you might say it's "something I've always wanted to do." If you do sail, be sure to say just enough to show empathy. Remember the 4-to-1 rule.

Let's face it; it's very tempting to talk about yourself and your own interests. Fight it. The more *response*-ability you demonstrate, the more successful you will be.

Building Trust

At this point, the prospect should be more comfortable with you as a person. You've shown an interest in what the prospect is interested in, you've mirrored him or her, and the prospect may have shared some personal information with you. Now it's time to learn about the prospect's business values.

An easy first question to ask is, "How long have you been with the company?" That question leads to, "Where were you employed previously?" and finally, "What's most important to you in your position?"

Once you know the answer to that key question, you will be better equipped to structure an effective presentation.

A great salesperson is smart, creative and has a positive mental attitude. He/she is a self-starter who has a high energy level, continually takes the initiative and consistently employs the basic selling skills and techniques on every call every day . . . and having a great sense of humor helps, too.
—Allen Dunstan, Vice President, Eastern Region, Newspapers First

Since you are currently at the point where most people begin, look how far ahead of the others you now are. Your prospect has shared so much with you that he no longer views you as a stranger who came there to sell something, but as someone who knows, likes, and understands him. The prospect is, therefore, more receptive to whatever you have to say next. The person's defenses are dissolving.

Keep your prospects talking. And remember that you should do no more than 25 percent of the talking on the appointment. Stick with the 4-to-1 Rule and your prospects will see you in a very special way.

BE YOURSELF

Be yourself. If you are self-effacing about your shortcomings, your prospects will relax in your company. For example, I'm a fumbler. I admit it. Even if I've put all my material at my fingertips in perfect order, I always seem to have a terrible time retrieving exactly the right piece at exactly the right time. Rather than ignoring this pause in the flow, I always call attention to my klutziness. I might make an off-the-cuff remark such as, "You know, I graduated from the Lucille Ball Academy of Material Retrieval."

This type of "I'm not as smooth as you" patter is guaranteed to be disarming. Use it to your advantage.

A great salesperson has perseverance, intelligence, and a relentless desire to succeed.

—Chad Brown, General Manager, WCBS Radio, Infinity Broadcasting

> I once met with the marketing director of one of New York's most elite hotels and his agency account executive. In his elegant office, he had a set of exquisite antique chairs. During the course of reaching for some sales materials and neglecting to notice that the chairs were on casters, my chair slid out from under me and I ended up seated very ungracefully on the floor. This bit of unintended slapstick provoked a lot of good-natured laughing from everyone . . . including me . . . and bonded us forever.
>
> Several years later, in responding to some updated sales information I had sent, the marketing director invited me over, with a parenthetical reference to having "secured the chairs." Obviously, this guy was on my side. (And he bought again.)

Differentiating the Male and Female Buyer

Male and female are really two cultures, and their life experiences are utterly different.

—Kate Millet, feminist author of *Sexual Politics*

As we have said before, it's our responsibility to get people to want to buy rather than to sell to them; and they like to buy the way in which they are most comfortable.

In his book *Men Are from Mars, Women Are from Venus,* John Gray makes the point that women and men have different styles of behavior. It will come as no surprise to most women that men prefer not to be helped. In general, they like to figure things out for themselves. If a man becomes lost while driving on a road, he most likely will want to find his way by himself rather than stop and ask for directions. Therefore, women should, in general, avoid using the word *help* when relating to men.

Men usually prefer not to shop around. If you can offer them a package that you know is competitive, you may have an opportunity to preempt other salespeople.

MALE AND FEMALE BONDING

Men can use male bonding to their advantage in making their "guy prospects" feel more comfortable. It is not difficult to find common ground on which to build a conversation: sports, women, movies, outdoor activities, cars . . . you know, the usual guy stuff.

A great salesperson knows how to sell understanding.

Phil Guarascio, former Vice President, General Motors

Women can also bond with female prospects to make them feel comfortable. Women usually find fashion, love, family, and sometimes men easy topics to talk to each other about. One can learn a great deal about a prospect's values from these discussions. Remember, however, that these gender-based observations are generalities, and as I was taught in school, we must beware of "glittering generalities."

THE OPPOSITE SEX

Of course, it often works to the salesperson's advantage to be the opposite sex. After all, women usually find men more exciting and vice versa. In a responsible, professional manner, we can all subtly harness this primal power to our advantage and make the other person feel special. You do it all the time. Don't keep the gender card hidden in the deck. Play it.

In summary, gender should be recognized, understood, valued, and respected in the quest for common ground.

Using Body Language—It Speaks Eloquent Volumes

I was once told in a job interview that I had great body language. It was a wonderful compliment. How you stand, sit, lean, and use your hands can add tremendous octane to your engine. It's also important to watch and interpret the other person's body stance and movements.

GOOD BODY LANGUAGE OVERCOMES BARRIERS

Beware the arm fold! When your prospect or client has folded arms, it means only one thing: There's a barrier between the two of you. Something you are doing, saying, or projecting is bothering that person. Use every jaws-of-life technique in your repertoire to get those pincers pried open. A person with folded arms is not favorably disposed to what you are offering. And you should never fold your own arms—except as a mirroring technique.

To pry open the arms, make sure that you let the person speak or vent without interruption. Often people let down their defenses after they speak their mind. Also, ask open-ended questions. Find out what might be the problem. Change the subject of the conversation.

Tip: Here are some other quick but important body language tips: Lean forward to emphasize a point or to show that you are listening intently. Within reason, keep eye contact. Don't forget to use your mirroring techniques.

Hands touching the face can indicate either thinking or showing concern. Be aware. There is more to communication than speech.

Since nearly 70 percent of communication is nonverbal, make sure your body language also sends the right message.

> I truly enjoy meeting people. I am fascinated by each new prospect I meet. I want to hear their ideas, know something about their world, and learn what's important to them. Most people seem to find my interest in them irresistible. And so, they tend to like being with me.

Your Tool Kit Is Growing

Give the lady what she wants.
> —Marshall Field, instructing the manager of his Chicago department store

For a person to buy from you and to feel that you are responsive, this person must feel you know him or her. If the prospect feels that you don't know where he or she is coming from, there will be a barrier that blocks an open channel to communication.

The best salesperson explains to me why they have the best value.
> —John McGowan, President, Trailer Bridge, Inc.

On the other hand, once you learn how the person processes information, which we will speak more about in the next chapter, you will be confident and self-assured in communicating. You will no longer worry about: How do I look? How do I sound to this person? Do I seem professional? Will this person think I'm intelligent? If the prospect senses little or no tension and a demeanor of openness and self-assurance coming from you, then he or she will respond in kind.

Up to now, our persuasion tool kit contains the following:

- ☛ Binary understanding of responsibility, which includes having a sense of *responsibility* and *response*-ability

☛ The power of observation

☛ Mirroring

☛ Knowledge of sensory behavior

☛ Knowledge of visualizers, auditories, and kinesthetics (V.A.K.s)

☛ Awareness of gender-based differences and similarities

☛ Knowledge of body language

There is one more vital tool that I use in my kit. It is invaluable for building a sense of trust through understanding. I call it the "Super Theory of *Relate*-tivity." It is the subject of Chapter 3.

using the super theory
of *relate*-tivity

SUCCESSFUL communication can be a very complex process. So, I'm going to simplify the process for you the way I do for myself.

It's really a matter of style. When processing information, each of us does it a bit differently. So, in order to successfully communicate information, you need to understand the information processing style of the person sitting across from you.

For example, if you are a wheat farmer and bring your crop (no matter how exceptional in quality) to a corn-processing facility, you're definitely going to get unsatisfactory results. Your crop will probably be rejected. But even if it's accepted, you're going to get an unusable finished product.

To put it another way, a computer with a Mac operating system can communicate with a Windows PC system *only* when they have been properly programmed to "understand" each other.

Show me a secure salesperson and I'll show you a poor salesperson. Successful salespeople are insecure, so insecure that they feel that the last thing that they've sold is the last thing they're ever going to sell. One of their biggest assets is a healthy fear of failure. It's that fear that drives them to push as hard as they can to succeed.

—Ira Ellenthal, EVP, Associate Publisher, *The New York Daily News*, and author of *Selling Smart*

Most people are only comfortable dealing with people who are like them. Furthermore, because they *treat* everyone else as if they were like themselves, they miss communicating well with approximately 75 percent of the people who are different.

When I was a teacher, for example, I realized that I was naturally more drawn to the students who were most like me: verbal, outgoing, warm, and so forth. I knew that it was my responsibility to relate to and help *all* my students to learn, including the ones who were quiet, withdrawn, and needed me to write things out for them.

That's when my Theory of *Relate*-tivity began to evolve from pure instinct into a structured system. Here's how it works.

First, Take Their Temperature

A great salesperson is one who knows how to establish rapport immediately, find out specifically what the prospect wants, needs, or has problems with, helps them get it quickly and elegantly (even if it's with another company), and has the prospect feel good about the product or service, the company, and them.

—Brian Azar, President, The Sales Doctor

When you meet someone, you can usually sense immediately whether the person is "warm" or "cool." The way you respond to this person is determined by this initial impression.

It's that simple. No matter how detailed and scientific we become in examining types of individuals, you will almost always be on target with this basic classification. For example, I think that most people would probably categorize Bill Clinton as a "warm" person and Al Gore as a "cool" person. Similarly, George W. Bush . . . warm . . . Dick Cheney . . . cool. Think about your friends and family. They are all wonderful people, of course, but some are wonderful and warm and some are wonderful and more on the cool side.

The next step is also very simple. How do you discern enough information about a complete stranger to be able to gain the person's confidence in the first few minutes of your acquaintance? Difficult you say? Actually, it's elementary, my dear facilitator. As you'll see next, you simply employ *observation* and *deduction*.

Next, Are They "New York" or "L.A.?"

When you first meet someone, you need to determine whether the person is a "New York" or an "L.A." person. Is the person forceful, dynamic, and always in a hurry, or is the person laid back, thoughtful, and receptive?

Then, Begin Typecasting

There are all types of people in your life. I've boiled them down to four basic iconic types. Some are naturally outgoing, chatty, and demonstrative. Others are no-nonsense, get-to-the-point people. Some are introspective thinkers, while others are warm, fuzzy, and sociable.

Your prospect is similar to one of those types. For the sake of illustration, I've selected four celebrity icons to represent the four basic types. You can use them for your own observation and deduction (O&D) and then substitute your own friends, relatives, acquaintances, or celebrity choices.*

THE OPRAH TYPE

She's a dynamo who is always full of energy. She uses her entire body when she talks, but especially her hands—for emphasis. Her voice covers the entire range from high to low, and she tends to speak somewhat loudly and quickly. She's a talker more often than an asker.

TIPS FOR RELATING TO THE OPRAH TYPE

She wants to tell you about her needs. Let her. She loves things that are creative, new, different—things that reflect her own enthusiasm. She wants the "big picture." Offer her incentives, but don't confuse her with options. Stroke her ego. Let her take the lead, but make it clear that you're there to help her achieve her vision.

When she gets angry, she may attack you. Everything is personal with her. Don't get ruffled or take her gruff attitude personally; that's her way when things don't work out the way she likes them.

THE AL ROKER TYPE

He is warm, friendly, and interested. He asks: "Where are you from? What do you like? Who do you know?" He's open, charming, and conversational. He's a social animal.

TIPS FOR RELATING TO THE AL ROKER TYPE

Work on establishing a relationship. He'll share his feelings. You should share information rather than give it. For example, let's say

* The celebrity names utilized herein are for illustrative and editorial purposes only, not to attempt to imply or denote false authorship, sponsorship, or endorsement nor to create any misleading claim or association as to the source or content of this work.

you have numbers and facts which you feel strongly indicate that what you offer is exactly what a prospect who is The Al Roker Type needs to achieve a particular goal.

By saying, "I have numbers and facts which show such and such . . . ," you will make this type of person feel under pressure, and because hard numbers and facts seem "cold" to his warm personality, you'll be turning him off.

Instead, you say something like, "This situation reminds me of a client who found himself in a similar position last year. He decided to try this particular solution and ended up being very successful."

This approach creates the feeling of sharing information and the idea of consensus, both of which appeal to The Al Roker Type.

The Al Roker Type likes getting his information in a warm, soft manner. Don't force feed him. Take your time. Make your point in an indirect manner.

The Al Roker Type will richly reward you with trust and positive inclinations. He needs to feel secure that others in his company will agree with his decision before he commits. Encourage their involvement.

Beware: He is so friendly that he hates to say no and could go to great lengths to avoid it. Don't expect quick decisions from The Al. Take time to gain his agreement, since he probably is asking others for their okay. Don't try to corner him.

It was one of the rules, which above all others, made Dr. Franklin the most amiable man in society: never contradict anybody.
—Thomas Jefferson

THE DONALD (NOT DUCK) TYPE

He is a just-the-facts kind of guy. He needs to feel in control. He only wants to know what he needs to know. For example, let's say you have the same numbers and facts that you had for The Al Roker Type. You are just as certain that they strongly indicate that what you have to offer is exactly what this prospect, The Donald Type, needs to achieve a particular goal.

If you even begin to "tell a story" as you did with The Al Roker Type, The Donald Type will cut you off at the knees. He is not as patient. Show him the numbers. Give him the facts. Use graphs, charts, and tables.

He's as closed as The Oprah Type is open. He offers few gestures or expressions. He provides little eye contact. He uses clipped tones and one-word answers. He won't let you know what he's thinking.

TIPS FOR RELATING TO THE DONALD TYPE

Be direct and to the point, not chatty. Talk return on investment or results, objectives, costs versus quality. Give him options to choose from. Let him be in control.

When he gets annoyed, let him vent. The issue is usually about the task at hand and not about you.

Neutron Jack [the name says it all]
—The nickname of Jack Welch, former CEO of General Electric

THE EINSTEIN TYPE

He asks: "What do you mean by that? How did you get that number? I'll have to think about it." You can almost hear his brain ticking, but you can't always follow where it's going. He's a *questioner*. He'll listen quietly, then ask questions quietly and usually slowly.

TIPS FOR RELATING TO THE EINSTEIN TYPE

Give him numbers, details, and facts. Put your proposal and ideas in writing. Be systematic and methodical. Give him time and space to make his decisions.

He reacts poorly to pressure and often asks for more paperwork. He likes to be asked questions and give his opinion. You must be prepared, efficient, and business-like when dealing with The Einstein Type.

✳   ✳   ✳

Everyone you meet will be a combination of these four icons. There will be one dominant quality and descending indications of the others. (The Al Roker Type with a touch of The Einstein Type, or The Oprah Type with a bit of The Donald Type, and so on.)

Be aware that there are very few people who are purely one type of icon. More about that later in this chapter.

The Family Tree

To illustrate the relationships between the icons, I've assembled a simple family tree, as shown in Figure 3-1. This tree will help you to zero in on the temperature and style of your prospects.

The following exercises will help you to understand and practice my identification system. After you've become comfortably proficient, you will be amazed at how much it helps you to quickly and successfully relate to all types of people.

The Seating Chart Exercise

Imagine that you are having a formal dinner party. As you prepare your place cards, you must decide who sits with whom. We all know that putting the right people together can make a successful occasion, whereas putting the wrong people together can be a social disaster. Well, fuggeddaboudit!

We'll use our four icons (The Oprah Type, The Al Roker Type, The Donald Type, and The Einstein Type) as a microcosm of our guest list.

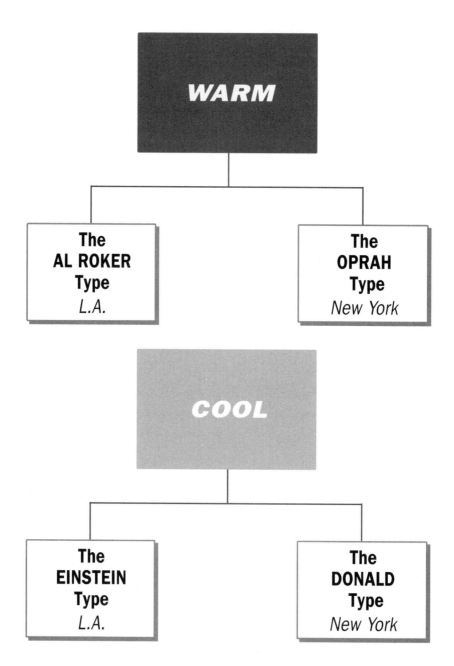

FIGURE 3–1 Family Tree

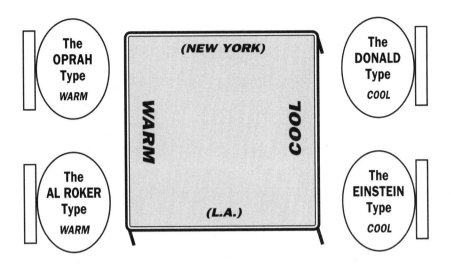

FIGURE 3-2 Ideal Seating Chart: warm with warm, cool with cool

So, first, let's take their temperatures. It's easy. The warm types are The Oprah Type and The Al Roker Type; the cool ones are The Donald Type and The Einstein Type.

Therefore, the ideal seating plan would be to put The Oprah Type and The Al Roker Type next to each other and The Donald Type next to The Einstein Type—that is, warm with warm and cool with cool.

However, if this ideal arrangement is not possible—and it often isn't—the next best arrangement would be to seat The Oprah Type with The Donald Type and The Al Roker Type with The Einstein Type—that is, New York with New York and L.A. with L.A.

How about The Al Roker Type with The Donald Type? Think about it: warm L.A. with cool New York. Bad idea! Would you seat The Oprah Type with The Einstein Type? That would be warm New York with cool L.A. Again, another bad idea.

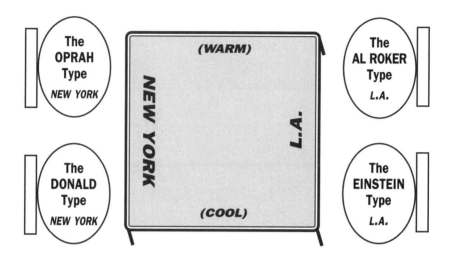

FIGURE 3–3 Second Best Seating Chart: New York with New York, L.A. with L.A.

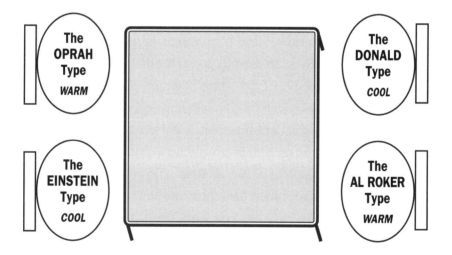

FIGURE 3–4 Worst Seating Chart: warm with cool, New York with L.A.

WHO ARE *YOU* MOST COMFORTABLE SITTING NEXT TO?

Know thyself *is never more important than in selling.*

—Harvey Mackay, motivational speaker, author of
Swim With the Sharks Without Being Eaten Alive

As the host of a social gathering, you need to relate to everyone. Are you warm or cool? New York or L.A.? The Oprah Type, The Al Roker Type, The Donald Type, or The Einstein Type? By now, you probably know exactly who you are. And if you're not sure, ask your friends and family. They'll tell you if you're the warm type or the cool type; the forceful New York type or the receptive L.A. type.

Of course, you'd prefer to sit next to someone who is most like you because it's more comfortable for you to relate to that person. Virtually no effort is required.

WHAT IF YOUR MATCH-UP IS LESS THAN IDEAL?

How do you relate to The Donald Type if you're The Al Roker Type, for example? Well, you do your best to do things in The Donald Type manner, that's how. The Donald Type wants choices. Therefore, you give The Donald Type choices. The Donald Type likes his ego stroked. So, you stroke his ego.

When you realize that you're The Al Roker Type and the other person is The Donald Type, you can adjust your approach to his style. You'll be very surprised by how even a little effort to do things the other person's way can pay big relationship dividends. It's the **Platinum Rule:** Do unto others as *they* want you to do unto them.

The concept of the Super Theory of *Relate*-tivity is simple. But the execution takes practice. Inertia tends to pull us toward the way we do things. So, we need to work diligently at shifting toward the way *other people—your prospects—*do things.

Tip: It's your responsibility to maximize your response-ability. I promise that with practice you'll be able to make every type of person feel very comfortable with you after a short time. When you observe, identify, adjust, and relate, you are guaranteed to succeed.

Once you know how to make a prospect feel comfortable, you can get the maximum out of the questioning process. You'll know how to ask for information in a manner most likely to make the prospect feel that you're primarily trying to help, not (ugh) sell.

Playing Identity Charades

A good way to practice identifying the different personality icons is to play the game of charades with an interested group.

Divide up into two teams. On individual slips of paper, write down the four icon types—The Oprah Type, The Al Roker Type, The Donald Type, and The Einstein Type—and place the names in a container. One team member, who plays the prospect, draws out a slip of paper that tells him or her which icon they'll be portraying.

By asking questions and observing reactions of the prospect, the rest of the team attempts to identify which personality type is being depicted. The team has sixty seconds to make its decision. The team is entitled to only one guess. If the team is correct, it receives two points; if the answer is incorrect, the other team gets one point. Right or wrong, the results should be discussed.

Now, it is the other team's turn to play. The first team to reach five points wins.

A Pop Quiz

The following table lists a series of traits. Match the traits to the corresponding icon type. *Note:* There may be more than one correct type match.

TYPES

A. The Oprah Type
B. The Al Roker Type
C. The Donald Type
D. The Einstein Type

TRAIT	TYPE
1. Speaks in clipped tones	
2. Uses hands a lot	
3. Avoids saying no to the salesperson	
4. Cares how others in the company will view his or her decision	
5. Wants to see written proposal	
6. Takes charge of the conversation	
7. Likes details	
8. Blames performance on the salesperson	
9. Hands usually closed	
10. Asks more questions	
11. Wants to see the big picture	
12. Uses direct eye contact	
13. Prefers to be given options	

14. May monopolize conversation

15. Responds to ego stroking

Answers: 1, C; 2, A; 3, B; 4, B; 5, D; 6, A or C; 7, D; 8, A; 9, C; 10, D or B; 11, A;12, A or B; 13, C; 14, A; 15, A or C

Assessing the Combinations

All of us are made up of a combination of the four iconic personalities. Although some people are almost "pure" types, most of us are *predominantly* one with *tendencies* toward others.

For example, you could be predominantly The Oprah Type, with tendencies toward The Al Roker Type. Or, you could be The Oprah Type with The Donald Type tendencies (Figure 3-5). You could be The Al Roker Type with tendencies toward The Oprah Type, or The Al Roker Type with The Einstein Type tendencies (Figure 3-6). You could also be The Donald Type with The Einstein Type tendencies, or The Donald Type with The Oprah Type tendencies (Figure 3-7). Finally, you could be The Einstein Type with The Donald Type tendencies. Or, alternatively, you could be The Einstein Type with The Al Roker Type tendencies.

As you can see, you can be a completely warm person and have either The Oprah Type or The Al Roker Type predominate. You're simply more New York or more L.A. Or, you can be a completely cool person and have either The Donald Type or The Einstein Type predominate. Once again, you're simply more New York or more L.A.

On the flip side, you could be a completely New York person with either The Oprah Type or The Donald Type predominating. Or, you could be a completely L.A. person with either The Al Roker Type or The Einstein Type predominating.

Meeting Yourself

You've probably had the most success with the personalities that are most similar to yours. You "know" them and are most comfortable approaching, working with, and selling to them.

Remember, however, that when under pressure, two Oprah Types, for example, are likely to attack each other personally, resulting in a negative experience. Be on guard for those moments and empathize with and give in to your prospect. Let the other person win.

If you and your prospect are both The Oprah Types and your prospect gets angry and attacks you, you'll know that is simply the

The Oprah Type   The Oprah Type/The Donald Type   The Oprah Type/
The Al Roker Type

FIGURE 3–5 The Oprah Type Combinations

The Al Roker Type   The Al Roker Type/The Einstein Type   The Al Roker Type/
The Oprah Type

FIGURE 3–6 The Al Roker Type Combinations

person's form of behavior. Do not take it personally. After all, that is just how The Oprah Types let others know they're angry or feeling under pressure.

Here is another example of meeting "yourself": If Donald Trump needs something from New York mayor and fellow billionaire Michael Bloomberg, then Mr. Trump needs to allow Mayor Bloomberg to feel that he (the Mayor) is in control of the situation. He can do this by offering His Honor a choice of acceptable options, by showing that he is listening carefully, and by letting Mayor Bloomberg do most of the talking.

Or, if you're a cool New York individual meeting another cool individual, albeit an L.A. type, what would you do? If Mr. Trump were meeting with bankers of The Einstein Type model, he would need to spell out every detail of his proposals and provide in-depth back-up materials. He would need to suppress his natural directing tendencies and ask more questions—as well as listen as empathetically as he can.

For all iconic personalities under pressure:

☛ Be aware of their style.

☛ Empathize with them, don't be defensive; let them attack or withdraw and then, with understanding, lead them out of their pressured state by *allowing them to speak.*

☛ Listen and don't interrupt; don't argue.

☛ Reassure them that you care.

☛ Help them clarify exactly what is bothering them.

☛ Try to solve the problem at hand.

The Einstein Type   The Einstein Type/The Donald Type   The Einstein Type/
The Al Roker Type

FIGURE 3–7 The Einstein Type Combinations

The Donald Type   The Donald Type/The Einstein Type   The Donald Type/
The Oprah Type

FIGURE 3–8 The Donald Type Combinations

Adjusting to Your Opposite Style

If you focus your attention and effort only on those people who are like you and with whom you feel comfortable, you could be missing out on more than 50 percent of your sales. That's a lot of lost sales!

Remember, if you are The Einstein Type, play to The Oprah Type's ego. Tell her about the sizzle and leave out the details until you meet another of The Einstein Type. If you're The Oprah Type, *puleeze* give The Einstein Type those details in writing that he so desperately needs. And slow down so that The Einstein Type can assimilate the information you gave him.

If you're The Donald Type, don't be so quick to get to the point when you're dealing with The Al Roker Type . He's a relationship kind of person. You need to find out who is important to him in the decision-making process. And if you're The Al Roker Type , forget about what is important to you and concentrate on what is important to The Donald Type . Get to the point, be direct, and give The Donald Type some choices in the matter. He or she doesn't care about relationships, but does care about the task at hand and being in charge.

What Type Is the Toughest for You to Relate To?

Of course, in the quick assessment of a prospect, you might discover that your qualities are in conflict with those of the other person.

If you're predominantly The Al Roker Type, you're going to have the *most* difficulty relating to The Donald Type . However, the more that The Donald Type has tendencies toward The Einstein Type or The Oprah Type , the easier it will be for you.

Conversely, if you're predominantly The Donald Type, you'll have the most difficulty relating to The Al Roker Type. But the more that he or she has tendencies toward The Einstein Type or The Oprah Type, the easier it will be for you.

People who are predominantly The Oprah Type have the most difficultly with people who are predominantly The Einstein Type, and less difficulty with people with tendencies toward The Donald Type or The Al Roker Type.

Finally, if you're predominantly The Einstein Type, you'll have the most difficulty with The Oprah Type, but less difficulty with people tending toward The Donald Type or The Al Roker Type.

Needless to say, it's vital for you to recognize the qualities of your prospect in relation to your own qualities so that you can be more *response*-able on their behalf.

Once you've practiced and mastered the Super Theory of *Relate*-tivity, you'll be in a position to apply the Platinum Rule to your prospects and *treat them as they wish to be treated.* They'll feel more comfortable with you. They'll put up fewer barriers. They'll trust you to keep *their* best interests as your primary goal.

The result? You'll be more successful.

In the 1980s, I was selling television time for an affiliate station in Philadelphia, KYW TV, Channel 3. While at a television and radio advertising conference, I began discussions with the general sales manager of the top-rated television station in town. We had met informally several times previously, and since I was constantly outselling his people, I thought he was aware of my professional abilities. He seemed to be very interested in me and asked me to send him a résumé. I was insulted. Surely, I thought, he knew enough about my qualifications from my reputation and I didn't bother to send a résumé. Why should I? To my astonishment, I never heard from him again.

In retrospect, I believe I know what happened. I was following the Golden Rule: *Do unto others as you would have them do unto you,* instead of the Platinum Rule.

I now know that in this case, I was The Oprah Type dealing with my opposite, The Einstein Type. Although I didn't realize it at the time, he needed that piece of paper with my résumé on it in order for me even to exist to him. No résumé. No Carol Super.

I believe that if I had sent the résumé as he asked, I would have landed that job.

Learn from Your Discomfort

As with most things in life, a good salesperson learns from adversity and will always try to "make lemonade out of lemons." Therefore, I am always working on developing those areas of my personality that are weakest in my "opposite" icon and that make me the most uncomfortable. By using the procedures outlined in this chapter, you will be able to develop a keen awareness of—and probably an appreciation and respect for—the strengths of your opposite so-called personality.

I'm the Oprah Type, therefore:

- I have *few adjustments* to make when dealing with another of The Oprah Type.

- I have *very little difficulty* adjusting to The Al Roker Type, because he is warm like me.

- I have *a bit more difficulty* adjusting to The Donald Type because he's cool, but he is still an assertive New York type like me.

- I have *the most difficulty* adjusting to The Einstein Type, because he is both cool and an L.A. type.

As The Oprah Type, I know I need to be able to comfortably check my emotions. Whenever I relate to someone who is an opposing icon, such as The Einstein Type (or for that matter, The Donald Type), I speak in a direct manner, not only to make *the other person* more comfortable but also to help keep *me* focused on the objectives set for our meeting. Otherwise, I can find myself off on a tangent; and before I know it, my allotted time is up and I'm nowhere.

I also have realized the value of The Einstein Type's strengths, such as being detail-oriented, and so I force myself to pay more attention to details. Often, when I am more detail-oriented, I find that I receive the recognition that The Oprah Types crave. I have learned to appreciate the watchword of The Einstein Type's faith, "God is in the details." And, I stop being upset about the need to write it all out.

Conversely, The Einstein Types could cultivate the benefits of The Oprah Type's assertiveness by tempering their excessive contemplation with action. They could also take more calculated risks because, after all, their natural sense of preparation has increased their chances for success.

The Al Roker Types will be more successful if they practice taking the initiative and setting goals the way that The Donald Types do. The Al Roker Types could also gain by appreciating the value of subordinating relationships to the task at hand, when necessary.

The Donald Type can learn from The Al Roker Type's great strengths of listening and knowing the value of interdependence in achieving goals. The Donald Types can gain not only from listening but also from acknowledging other people's viewpoints.

A Game of Personality Role-Playing

From a container, pick out a slip of paper with the name of an iconic role for a prospect to assume. Then, from another container, pick an item that you want that prospect to buy, such as:

- A Jaguar automobile

- A personal computer

- A popcorn maker

- An antique table

- A player piano

- A 300-channel satellite dish system

Assume that you have a qualified, interested, and desirous buyer in front of you. Be imaginative in creating product benefits that match the personality's type. Make your presentation in a manner that makes the icon type trust you and buy from you.

My father was a brilliant car dealer and used to tell me that men came into his showroom saying that they wanted good basic transportation, but when they brought their wife in wearing a fur coat, it was obvious that they needed something that enhances their image too.

Spending the time to read the customers' needs is the right way to make an effective sale. Then serve up your product or service as a solution to those needs. But, at the end of the day, if you don't like people, you shouldn't be selling. A great salesperson has a genuine and expressed desire to help solve a problem for the customer. They focus on what the customer really needs, what their gut-wrenching issue is (it's not always what they say they need).

—Lynne Seid, Chief Client Officer, EVP, BBDO Advertising Agency

Relating vs. Relationships

Now, let's look at the distinction between the terms *relating* and *relationships*. They're not the same.

Think about these two statements:

"In order to have a relationship, you need to relate."

"In order to relate, you don't necessarily need a relationship."

What are the implications of these two statements? Many sales-people and their managers feel that relationships are everything, while critics of this philosophy say that relationships don't mean better sales or buyer loyalty. The truth, however, is that they are both right.

It is simply a matter of knowing when you should relate by building relationships and when you should relate simply by helping the buyer reach his or her objectives. Of course, relating can develop later into a relationship, but it shouldn't be forced.

I once had a sales manager who insisted that making or not making a sale was "all in the relationship." Unlike the game of golf, where they say that "it's all in the wrist," my practical experience showed me that relationships were *not always* important to the buying decision. Sometimes they were critical, sometimes they tipped the balance, and sometimes they simply didn't matter much at all.

My advice is to not let relationship building divert you, because relationship building is a tool, not an objective.

You're OK, I'm OK, But Not as OK as You Are (with apologies to the late Eric Berne)

No one likes to be intimidated. So, we don't want to make our prospects feel intimidated. This doesn't mean we should be wimps. We should, however, *develop the skill of letting the other person feel comfortably in control.* After all, it is important to remember that we're encouraging a buying decision, which, of course, is in the prospect's control.

By helping the prospect to win, you win. How do you accomplish this subtle feat? You don't need to literally let the prospect win by losing yourself. It is more about how you play the game. When renowned golf pro Greg Norman and Bill Clinton played golf together in Australia, there was no question about who would get the better score.

Norman, however, put President Clinton at ease by making him feel good about his game, giving him lighthearted pointers, and making the whole experience fun, interesting, and worthwhile, rather than competitive.

Similarly, it's up to you to remove any feeling of competition between you and your prospect. It is usually counterproductive to let your natural competitiveness show. The superslick, impeccably dressed, highly polished, seemingly "perfect" salesperson can make the buyer feel inadequate, which sets up a buyer's defensiveness and, consequently, a potential conflict.

Dressing appropriately isn't cut-and-dried, however. The definition of proper business attire is murky these days. Some offices are suit-and-tie, whereas others are dress-down casual. Some are casual only certain days of the week. It can be difficult to develop well-defined rules for your own dress other than to be clean, well-groomed, with clothes pressed, shoes highly polished, and professionally dressed in a manner that makes you feel comfortable and confident. Just be sure that if your outfit runs counter to the office you're entering, address that fact.

If you seem overdressed, perhaps make reference to "having to be in uniform for another meeting." If underdressed, make an excuse such as, "My luggage got lost." This should diffuse any discomfort on either side.

Speaking of keeping people comfortable, I have been teased, on occasion, by my management and even by clients who have bought from me, about my being slightly uncoordinated, as I've mentioned before. Using this natural imperfection has actually served me quite well. It makes others feel a little more comfortable about themselves. I've always felt that this was the reason I was named "class wit" in my school yearbook. After all, I did make them laugh.

Wrap-Up to Relating

A diplomat is a man who always remembers a woman's birthday, but never remembers her age.

—Robert Frost

We've covered the essential first step in influencing a prospect to buy. By now, your prospects should feel that they are talking to someone who understands them and sincerely has their best interests at heart. They now see you as someone with whom they would like to do business. All that remains is for you to show them that what you offer can make a positive difference in their lives.

In subsequent steps, you'll be able to make use of the tools you now have. You now know how the prospect processes information on a sensory, emotional, and, thus, an intellectual level.

Before you can give prospects information to process, you need to find out what is important to them—what they perceive their needs to be—and to do it in such a way that it *reveals a need for what you're offering*. This may sound like a tall order, but once again, it's just a matter of understanding the process.

You can feel confident that you've now created a strong foundation with your prospect. Let's build on it.

steps 3 to 4½ : the process

inquiry, presentation, and the close

harnessing the
power of inquiry

ONE OF THE TRICKS that most magicians know is called "forcing a card." There are several methods of forcing a card. Here is a basic one called "the slip force." Through a simple sleight-of-hand move during a slow riffle, the magician slips a card *that he has already glimpsed* into a specific place in the deck where the spectator has said, "Stop." When the spectator "chooses" that card, he or she is actually selecting the forced card. Since the magician already knows the card, he can now reveal it in any manner he chooses. Voila! The spectator is amazed. The magician is amazing. The deck was "stacked."

In this section we're going to describe how I "stack the deck" on a sales call in order to "force" a buying decision, while making the prospects feel that it was their choice alone; therefore, one that they feel very comfortable with. There is nothing sinister in this process. We are responsible for *making their lives better;* and if you sincerely feel what you have to offer will do that, then it's *your responsibility* to help in any way to make it happen.

Simple Background Questions

Three qualities are essential to being a great salesperson: the first one is listen to the customer. The second one is really listen to the customer. The third one is really and sincerely listen to the customer.

—Gerhard Gschwandtner, Publisher, *Selling Power*

The process begins with your asking simple background questions. First, ensure that the prospect knows that in order to explain your product or service in a manner that will best serve him, you need his permission to ask a few questions. For example, you might ask, "Do you mind if I take a few notes?"

The purpose of making these *soft inquiries* is both to obtain useful information and to further put the prospect at ease. And you don't need to worry about your responses to their answers. Since the questions require no quantifiable answers that could be challenged in any way, the focus stays comfortably on the prospect. These soft warm-up questions keep the conversation flowing and allow prospects to give their point of view. Everyone likes to be asked for and to give her point of view. Your interest also reinforces the feeling that the prospect is a little more okay than you are.

These simple questions also serve as a comfortable transition from the *relating phase* to this *inquiry phase.* Sample warm-up background questions might include:

- How long have you been with the company?

- Where were you employed previously?

- What do you like best about the company?

The key background question is: What is most important to you in your position? The prospect's answer to that key question:

- Gives you the focus you need in structuring your presentation

- Gives you valuable information about the client's personal needs

- Reinforces the personality quadrant in which you've mentally placed the prospect

- Helps you to effectively plan your questions during the next inquiry phase

The "Retrieving the Facts" Phase

What makes a great salesperson? Ears. The best salespeople listen and offer what you need, not what they have."

—Geoff Klapish, Vice President, Media Director, Hill Holiday Advertising

I find the inquiry phase to be the most challenging and rewarding aspect of the persuasion process. You're asking a series of comfortable questions, the answers to which give you vital factual information to help you determine the problems the prospect may have and provide you with the basis for your next question.

As in tennis, the way you "return" the question depends on how it is "hit" to you.

Remember, your goal during the inquiry phase is to hold up a mirror to prospects' needs and, through skillful questioning, move the context of the answers to their needs toward your product or service. Skillful questioning will reveal, in their own words, how your product or service will meet those needs.

When a prospect asks you a question during your inquiry, reply with another question. At this point, you don't want to give answers—you want to get answers. For example, if you are asked, "Does your product come in blue?", your response should be, "Oh, is color an important consideration? Why is that?"

Be patient. The process of revealing how your product or service meets the prospect's needs should not begin until *after* you have established as many needs as you can. Only then can your questions and the prospect's answers be solution-oriented.

Jumping the gun will only tip your hand and cause you to lose control before you have fully established the value of your product. In the Sandler Selling system course, taught by Brian Azar, the Sales Doctor, this is referred to as "spilling your candy in the lobby."

Three dangers of leaping to solutions too early are:

1. Being taken where you don't want to go

2. Not getting needed information

3. Taking the focus off the client and putting it back on you

The following is an example of what can happen when you help the prospect reveal a need and then *immediately* attempt to show how your product or service can meet it:

"How many people do you currently have who use a laptop computer?"

"Right now, forty-seven."

"Would it be easier for them to do business when they are traveling if they were able to send a fax from their computer without having to plug into a phone line?"

"You mean they won't have to search around for a phone jack? That sure is a hassle."

"So hunting for a phone jack wastes a lot of time?"

"I'll say! When I was in Jersey City yesterday, I spent nearly two hours searching before I found one, and it almost cost me a contract."

"One of the features of our new Series 1620 computers is wireless access. You can send a wireless fax from anywhere there's cellular service."

"Wow—that sounds great! Is it available now?"

"It sure is."

"How much does it cost?"

"The new 1620 Series starts at $6,700 a unit."

"$6,700!! You must be kidding. I'd rather take my chances with a phone jack."

No sale! What happened here?

First, the seller allowed the prospect to jump to the price before the true value of the product had been established, thereby closing off any possibility of further advancing the sale by revealing other needs. The seller has been propelled into the "red alert" or "damage control" mode.

The following scenario shows how the inquiry conversation might have been guided to ensure a positive outcome:

"How many people do you currently have who use a laptop computer?"

"Right now, forty-seven"

"Would it be easier for them to do business when they are traveling if they were able to send a fax from their computer without having to plug into a phone line?"

"You mean they won't have to search around for a phone jack? Because that sure is a hassle."

"So hunting for a phone jack wastes a lot of time?"

"I'll say! When I was in Jersey City yesterday, I spent nearly two hours searching before I found one, and it almost cost me a contract."

"That must have been scary. Does this kind of thing happen often?"

"Our people are on the road a lot. They may spend two weeks a month away from home, and I guess this happens to them at least a couple of times each trip."

"You mean at least four times a month?"

"That's probably right."

"Does this hassle ever actually cost your company business?"

"I'm afraid so."

"Wow, that *is* scary!"

"Yep, and it doesn't make me look too good to my boss, either."

"Having to search for a phone jack causes your people to lose a lot of important time, on occasion business, and has the potential for your company to really lose a major contract."

"It could happen."

"If you had to put a rough dollar value on the loss of time, the hassles, and the potential business losses, what do you think that might be over a year?"

"Oh, I'd have to say it could be a up to $10,000 or more a person."

"Then, that might come to roughly $250,000 to $500,000? Let's say a half-million dollars in losses."

"Possibly."

"How important is your e-mail network in your business?"

"With forty-seven salespeople, e-mail is essential."

"In what ways is it essential?"

"Well, in our business, prices are constantly fluctuating and a few cents either way could make a big difference; so they need to have access to their e-mail for real-time quotes."

"How's that going?"

"Not that great, because they're often being asked to give bids on the spot and they may be away from a phone jack."

"Sounds like that could cost you too."

"I'm afraid so."

"Roughly, how much does this cost you a year?"

"Oh, I'd have to say, again, about $10,000 a person in round numbers. Yeah, and that doesn't look so good on my bottom line. I always get questioned on that."

"What you're saying is that simply because your people have to search for phone line access for their computers, it could be costing your company in excess of a million dollars a year?"

"I guess that is what I'm saying."

"It certainly seems that your company could benefit from a computer with a wireless access feature."

"Yes, if it existed. Are you saying it does?"

"Yes, our new Series 1620 has that feature built in."

"No kidding?" How much do they cost?"

"It depends. There are several new models that contain this feature and I need to know some of your other requirements to be able to suggest which model might serve you best."

As you can see from this scenario, the salesperson keeps the spotlight on the prospect's point of view, probes to find and clarify his needs, and allows the prospect to state his needs.

Developing Need Questions

Begin each call thinking of the dissatisfaction you can fill, and what questions you will need to ask to determine if it exists, and to what extent, or how you'll help them recognize any latent dissatisfaction.

—Art Sobczak, in his *Telephone Selling Report*

Begin by working backward. Take a benefit that your company offers and think of what dissatisfaction it eliminates for your prospect. Then write out the appropriate question you would ask. For example, let's say that you are selling the world's fastest copier. The questions you need to ask are: "How often do you find yourself frustrated by waiting for copies?" "How many important jobs are delayed?" "How much time is being wasted?" "How much is that time worth to your company?"

The salesperson knows where he or she wants the conversation to go, and so asks leading questions to establish need. When the prospect answers these leading questions, the needs are now put in the prospect's own words so that he or she can realize the significance of that need.

The salesperson then asks clarification questions to further enhance the importance of the prospect's needs. For example, the salesperson might ask: "What do you mean by essential?" "In what ways was it a 'hassle?'" "Then, what you are saying is . . ."

The next step is to be able to quantify the need, whenever possible, with a dollar value. You might say, "So, not having ready access to information is costing you more than 200 sales per month?" or "You're saying that a wireless system could mean another $50,000 or more in sales every year?" Finally, have the *prospect* state the benefits of the product.

By the end of the scenario, the prospect has "selected the card" the salesperson intended. He or she has found that your product is the answer to an important need. Notice, the salesperson has still not answered the price question. Until the product or service value has been established *to its fullest,* cost discussion should be postponed.

The inquiry step is really like following a path rather than a rigid system. It is up to you to know where you want to go and to guide, not push, the prospects to your destination by having them feel, as much as possible, that *they* found the way.

The Seven Signposts

There are issues questions that must be addressed to help you properly guide prospects and for prospects themselves to be aware of their needs:

1. *Examination of current marketing efforts and goals.* (If you don't know where they are presently, you certainly can't guide them to a new destination.)

2. *Competitive marketing efforts.* (How is your competition "eating your lunch"?)

3. *Satisfaction level.* (How much is not having _____ costing your company?)

4. *Seasonality.* (Is summer a key time for you?)

5. *Market demographics.* (Who are you going after? What is your target market?)

6. *Budgeting concerns.* (What is your budget allocation for this year? Has it increased? Are you on a calendar year budget?)

7. *Decision-maker(s).* (Who else is involved? Who are influencers? What will you need to do to win their support? How are decisions made in your company?)

Transforming Needs to Problems for Which You Have the Answers

Asking a so-called automatic question such as "How's it going?" will bring an automatic answer such as "Fine" or "Well" or "No problem." I operate under the *Rule of Three.* You usually need to ask three *specific* questions to uncover a need or to get the information you might need.

I was reminded of the effectiveness of the Rule of Three a few years ago when my mother had a serious heart attack. She was ninety-two at that time and instinctively knew how to get the right answers out of anyone about anything.

She had a choice of surgical procedures to repair the damage that her heart attack had caused, either open-heart surgery or angioplasty to open blocked arteries. Instead of making an arbitrary decision on a life-and-death matter, she asked the doctor, "What do you think I should do?" His answer was in the form of clinically sterile "doctor-ese" that only another medical person could possibly have understood.

So, Mom asked another question, this time a little more personal: "What would you do if you were me?" Since he was now thinking about himself, he answered with more unusable medical mumblings, but this time his words were delivered with more warmth.

Mom then smiled and said, "I remember going into your uncle's store when you were a very, very young man. He was so proud of you even then. Your whole family was always very proud of you. Tell me, doctor, if I were your mother, and you had to help her make this decision, what would it be?"

"Angioplasty," he said.

"Thank you," said my mother. And angioplasty it was. The procedure was very successful and gave my mother a new lease on life.

My mother actually might have invented the Rule of Three.

Let's continue with a difficult task—finding out your prospects' satisfaction level with their present circumstances, so that you know how to lead them to what you have to offer. To do that, you want to move from the general to the specific so that you end up with a *quantifiable* response. Let's look at two examples that illustrate this point. In the following scenarios, the salesperson is selling a targeted medium such as direct mail or a niche publication.

"Do you feel that you are reaching your [previously identified] target?"

"Not completely, but I feel we're doing a pretty good job."

"Pretty good job? Does that mean you're reaching at least 75 percent of your market?"

"Um, maybe 55 to 60 percent."

"Is one of your goals to increase that number?"

"I'd like that."

OR

"Do you feel you're reaching as much of your [previously iden-tified] target as possible?"

"I doubt we could afford that."

"When you say 'afford,' does that mean you're spending as much as you can on your mass media?"

"Yeah, that's right.

"How much of what you're spending is waste?" [Waste is the percentage of mass media dollars that miss the target market; for example, a man watching a bra commercial.]

"With our product, I'd say about 25 percent or so."

"Does that mean that 25 percent of your budget should be working harder to reach your target?"

"Yes, but the question is how?"

"First, let me ask you, 'What does 25 percent represent in dol-lars and cents to your budget?'"

"Oh, about a million and a half."

Let's analyze these two scenarios. The first question that was asked related to the previous discussion about the company's market. It was a specific question that would reveal a prospect's needs. Also, in the first scenario, the seller asked for a clarification of the vague description of "pretty good job," by leading the prospect to a quantifiable answer.

Tip: In the inquiry mode, always be aware of the need to clarify responses. Don't assume you know what a vague term means. Here are some examples of vague terminology:

☞ "A lot"

☞ "A little"

☞ "Too much"

☞ "Not exactly what we need"

☞ "Maybe"

☞ "Sort of"

☞ "The type of"

☞ "Doesn't quite fit"

☞ "More than we need"

☞ "Haven't decided"

☞ "Not sure about"

☞ "Later"

Ask for clarification and, whenever possible, quantification. Clarification is a vital component of the leading process.

In the second scenario, when the prospect answered, "I doubt I could afford that," the salesperson led him to realize that he had a need to obtain greater efficiency—which, of course, is what the salesperson is selling. The salesperson, by asking the right questions, also found out the specific media budget and the possible allocation for the product he is selling.

Lead the prospect from the general to the specific and in the direction of what you are selling. The prospect must become aware of his or her need and state what it is.

Determining the Budget

To properly serve a client, it is essential to know the size of his or her budget.

If you ask, "What is your budget?" without laying out the proper groundwork, your prospect will usually feel that you want to know the answer only so you can spend it all on what you're selling. If your prospect believes that you are there to help her, however, she will be much more likely to share this vital information with you. Say something such as, "So as not to waste your time by suggesting an unrealistic plan, I need to know in round numbers approximately how much is budgeted in this area."

Who Is the Decision-Maker?

In order for the first six signposts to have any value, it is essential that you identify the seventh: Who is the decision-maker?

A simple, nonthreatening way to get this information is to ask: "What's the decision-making process like in your organization?" The answer to this question will tell you where to go next, which could be to somebody else's office or to several other offices.

Be sure you find out everyone in the organization who is involved in the decision-making process—and in major accounts, cover them all!

How often have you thought you had it all wrapped up, only to have everything unravel because you had been wooing the wrong person or neglecting that person's boss or bosses? Many people may be involved in the decision-making process, but only one person can say yes in the end.

> My husband's advertising agency expended countless hours of work, rivers of sweat, and immeasurable creative energy preparing a campaign for a major hospital, with the input of its very cooperative and supportive marketing director. When the campaign was presented to the marketing director, she was ecstatic. "This is great! This is exactly what we need! It's warm. It's clever. It's memorable. I can't wait to show it to the general manager. Call me Monday and we'll get it started." Needless to say, in spite of wariness developed over years of preparing presentations, it was difficult for the agency to contain its excitement over the enthusiastic response to its work.
>
> When the agency called back Monday to "get started," a very contrite marketing director told them that the general manager had not liked the campaign. Boom! End of story. Wrong person. Big disappointment.

You simply can't get a favorable decision if you haven't reached the decision-maker.

How Are Decisions Made?

Let's say you are asking a prospect to buy something new. That could be scary and uncomfortable for him. If what you are offering doesn't fit into the "this is what we've always done" or "this is the way we've always done it" category, the prospect risks making a high-profile "mistake." Nobody wants to make a high-profile mistake.

Therefore, it is your responsibility to inquire about and understand the company's buying process to make things as easy as possible for the prospect.

What is the process for considering something new? Who is in charge? Who is in the loop? How is it brought up? How does the company like to obtain its information? How is the corporate culture set up to process the information?

You may be surprised to discover that when you ask questions such as *"How* do you buy?", *"When* do you buy?", or "From *whom* do you buy?", you'll often get a blank stare at first. This is because companies don't often microanalyze their buying processes. So by asking them to do so, you're actually helping them to think in a new direction. And that is exactly what you want them to do. You're benefiting in two ways: Not only are you getting vital information but you're also doing your prospect an important service for which he or she will be grateful.

More Leading Questions

As demonstrated in our previous inquiry scenarios, the following are the kinds of leading questions that will help clients reveal their needs to themselves and to *you,* for which you, of course, have an answer:

- Does that mean that . . .?

- What's the effect that . . .?

- Does that create . . .?

- That leads to . . .?

☞ Right?

☞ What does that mean to . . .?

☞ How much does that . . .?

☞ Doesn't that . . .?

☞ Is that . . .?

☞ Would it . . .?

☞ Wouldn't it . . .?

☞ Could that . . .?

☞ Couldn't that . . .?

Notice that this list of questions does not include any "why" questions, which are often perceived by the prospect as being confrontational. The prospect might feel as if she is being interrogated. For example, "Why did you choose your present vendor?" is a confrontational question, whereas "What was the process you used in making your choice of vendors?" is a nonconfrontational question.

Also, make certain that your question gives you an answer you can utilize. Rather than asking, "Is your present vendor doing a good job for you?", ask instead, "What do you like about your present vendor, and what more would you like to get from them, if you could?"

Finally, make certain your question is not invasive, such as, "So, what are you doing about the competition?" Ask instead, "Can you give me an idea of what you're planning to do to handle competitive pressures?"

Benefits Questions

Even after having prospects reveal their needs to you and to themselves, they still won't know definitely how your product or service
will be a solution for them because you're still establishing value. At
this point, the prospect must verbalize the benefits of what you're
offering to his or her company, even though the prospect doesn't
know yet exactly what it is that you're offering.

The following are examples of leading benefits questions:

- Why would this solution be useful?

- Is it important to solve . . .?

- How do you think this product or service would help you?

- How do you feel this product or service would benefit your
  company?

- What do you see this doing for you?

- What do you *feel* this will do for you?

- What does this *sound like* it could do for you?

- You'd be interested in saving money, reaching the right people, reducing time, correct?

- Is there any other way this could help you?

This last question not only can suggest other benefits to the
prospect but also might make the person aware of how your product
or service might be the solution to other needs he might not even

have been aware of up to now. Whereas the first group of questions is designed to reveal *needs,* the answers to this series of questions will reveal *benefits.*

Because the prospect is now doing the revealing with her answers, there will be fewer objections when you finally present your solutions. The simplest way to easily differentiate needs questions from benefits questions is that the answers to the benefits questions will be positive. For example:

Needs question: Which part of your investment portfolio is underperforming?
Benefits question: Would a free investment analysis be helpful to you?

Needs question: What is there about your present housing situation that you would like to change?
Benefits question: In your present circumstances, would a smaller home be more suitable?

At this point, instead of it being a giant step from their needs to your solutions, it's only a tiny step, which you can easily help prospects to take.

Isn't it amazing? You still haven't revealed much about your product or service, yet the prospect has virtually stated that it is exactly what he or she needs.

Congratulations! The "card" has been forced.

Recap

Here is what you have accomplished so far:

In Step 1, you developed a positive attitude and a strong sense of responsibility.

In Step 2, you related to the prospect and developed an understanding of how the person processes information.

In Step 3, through the inquiry phase, you asked the prospect a few background questions, and the key question, and then guided the person through the process of leading questions that led to specific answers to uncover his or her needs—and, whenever necessary, asked clarifying questions. Finally, you asked the prospect benefit questions to elicit positive responses and the prospect stated how helpful your product or service would be.

Now, give them what they're begging for, which is Step 4, the Presentation.

The prospect has identified his needs and now has an idea of what it takes to meet these needs. Of course, this is exactly what you're going to offer.

Always remember: The presentation step is not an island. It is a bridge to a close, which is Step 4½.

You must first decide if this is the right time and place to present. Is the decision-maker present? Are there time constraints? For example, is it lunchtime? Does the client have another meeting? Does he or she have to catch a train? Is your hour up?

Do you have all the necessary information or support people with you? Do you have any number crunching to do, based on information you just obtained?

In short, is it the right time? If so, then proceed to Step 4.

chapter 5

creating a successful presentation

BEFORE YOU MAKE your presentation, it is essential that you do a prepresentation review.

Prepresentation Review

First, review the information that your questioning process has induced the prospect to reveal. For example, you might say: "Here's what you've told me so far." Then, list the needs that you know your product or service will meet. Ask review questions, such as "Is that right?" The prospect will say yes, because you are essentially just repeating her words.

Tip: Do not omit the essential prepresentation review step. It's important to remind prospects of what they have just told you. This keeps the focus on *their needs,* as *they* have presented them, versus your telling them what they need. If you skip over this step, your presentation of the solution will lose most of its impact simply because of its distance from the statement of the need. You will have diminished instead of enhanced your position.

Initial Benefit Statement

At this point, be certain to give your prospect a taste of the primary *benefit* he or she is about to receive from your product or service, based on your review of the prospect's needs.

Some initial benefit statement (IBS) examples are: "I'm going to show you how my product will save you money" or "save you time," or "enhance employee motivation and morale" or "give you a major competitive edge."

Notice that the IBS is not a statement of product features, such as size, speed, options, and the like. It is an underscoring of the fulfilling of a major need that the prospect has indicated would make his life better. And remember, that is your job.

Your Presentation (Your Response)

Being a great salesperson comes from the following: confidence, expertise, passion, and patience—or C.E.P.P. In the art world, those who are not only successful but have stood the test of time are: Confident in themselves, Experts in their field, Passionate about their work, and above all, Patient with their clients.

—Howard L. Rehs, President, Rehs Galleries, Inc.

Relax. Contrary to what you may have been told, a presentation is by no means the most vital step in the buying process. In fact, your presentation shouldn't be a presentation. It should be a *response*.

There's a critical difference between a presentation and a response. Your presentation is probably a formal, preplanned, for-matted, scripted account of *all* that your product or service is. Some prospects will be patient and kind enough to sit through it. Some won't. All will be unsatisfied to some extent. That's because you're "making a pitch" and they're expected to respond. Everyone is uncomfortable.

But how else can you get your company's message across than giving the entire canned sales presentation?

The answer is to simply and only respond to the stated needs of the prospect. Since you've gone to the trouble of establishing the prospect's needs, it is important to focus on fulfilling those needs. Showing more than the prospect has stated he or she needs could completely ruin the rapport that you have so skillfully achieved.

Even though you'll be actively using only a part of your "prepared" presentation, you still must know it all cold. That's the only way you'll be able to select the precise portions that create the best fit for the prospect's needs and your solutions. You should use every possible weapon in your arsenal to meet the stated needs.

And by responding, not presenting, you will be demonstrating that your focus really is firmly on your prospect and that her trust in you as facilitator is warranted.

Although you might well choose to leave your entire presentation with prospects for review at their convenience, directly respond with only the specific information that they have indicated to you that they require.

Remember that your presentation should be perceived as a *recommendation*. The prospect should feel that it is part of his buying decision, not that something is being sold to him. At this stage, it is also important to remember the personality type to which you are making these recommendations:

- The Einstein Type needs you to provide specific written facts and figures.

- The Donald Type needs detailed information as well, but he or she also requires ego nourishment.

- The Oprah Type needs to see a vision of how your product or service meets their needs.

- The Al Roker Type should be shown what your product or service can do for the organization at large. You must demonstrate to The Al Roker Type how well he or she will be regarded for bringing your product or service to the company.

Since, as we said earlier, nearly 85 percent of the population is visually oriented, as much of your presentation as possible should be visual. Also, include auditory, tactile, and/or olfactory elements whenever you can, because people remember better when they use more than one of their senses.

Make the presentation fit the prospect's need. The following examples show how to do that:

- You said _____ (for example, *efficiency*) is important. I suggest you consider _____ (product/service).

☛ You mentioned improving _____ (let's say, *prestige*) was a key goal to your company; consequently, you might want to look at/hear about/feel the fit of the product or service.

Name the specific product or service—for example, Personalized Banking, the new M16 Cellular Modem, the Color-Magic 2000 Printer—rather than saying "our." You're instead suggesting a *specific answer* to the prospect's need.

Taking Their Temperature

Be sure to continually "take the prospect's temperature" as you are presenting, by asking the following questions:

"Does this look/sound/feel right for you?"

"Do you agree?"

"Is this what you meant by . . . ?"

"Have I missed anything?"

"Do you have any questions so far?"

As you can see, taking the prospect's temperature simply means asking how the person is doing. By asking how he or she is doing, you're keeping tabs on how you're doing—and you're building a solid bridge to the close.

In case you haven't noticed, we're still in the "creating the value" stage and, therefore, have not yet mentioned price. You're trying to move your product or service as much into the "must have" category as possible.

Recognizing Buying Signals: Stop, Caution, Go

Prospects project buying signals. Be very careful. Zooming through them toward the close could cause a crash and, therefore, fatal damage to the buying decision. Instead, recognize those signals and follow their messages to keep things moving smoothly.

THE STOP SIGNAL

It's amazing how many salespeople seem to be blind to this signal. When a prospect folds his or her arms and says something like, "Well, this sounds good but we can't do it right now," the reaction often is to take this signal as a "maybe" and press for a close. Wrong. Not only won't it happen, but driving through a stop signal also makes the prospect think that you're not paying attention—or that you're putting your best interests ahead of her interests. That instantly ruins any rapport, trust, and openness that you have so carefully developed and creates a disastrous adversarial position.

Be careful not to drive through a stop signal. *Stop.* Find out why there was a stop signal. Ask whether the prospect needs more information, or whether there is no budget, or whether it's the wrong season or they're in the midst of changing their marketing message, or whether others in the buying decision chain need to be consulted. The prospect will appreciate your recognizing and respecting his stop signal, and the professional relationship of trust you have built will continue.

My manager, Rob Reif, recently told the following story to a third party over lunch.

When I went out on my first call to an important prospect with Carol, we reached a point in our meeting when the client said, "Well, why don't you just run me some numbers on ten markets." I thought that was great and would have eagerly agreed to get her the information.

I must admit, I was really shocked when Carol said, "You know, Becky, I can see that you're not ready to buy right now. Whenever you are, please call me and I'll get you any information you need."

Carol had recognized the stop signal. The prospect had been simply giving us some "busy work" so that our trip to her office wouldn't be totally in vain. She thought she was being nice to us. But Carol had been paying attention to everything the prospect had been telling us during the meeting. She knew that now was not the time. The prospect was also taken aback—and impressed—by Carol's honesty and directness. Indeed, when the time was right, she called Carol and ended up as a substantial client. By recognizing that there was no go sign that day, Carol preserved a relationship of trust. That's the sign of a great salesperson.

THE GO SIGNAL

The go signals are much easier to see because we're looking for them. The prospect will say things such as, "What color is it available in? Are shipping costs included? When will you have these in stock? How soon can they be delivered?"

THE CAUTION SIGNAL

Some caution signals are: "This is great, but I have to run it by my general manager . . ." or "Sounds good, but I have to find some dollars in the budget . . . ." In other words, a positive reaction with a "but."

When you encounter a caution signal, simply proceed with caution. Review the benefits that have been established, offer any help you can, set up the next meeting, and move on.

When prospects say, "I want to think it over," proceed with caution. Review. Be sure that the prospects understand that the value of your product outweighs its cost. This will help keep them "thinking it over" in your favor.

Show your understanding. Take responsibility. Say, "I must not have given you enough information for you to make a decision. What more do you need?" You might even ask, "What do you need to think about?"

By looking for and recognizing a prospect's buying signals, you powerfully increase your opportunity for a positive buying decision. By ignoring the signals, you exponentially decrease your chances.

PRICE

If the timing is right, just give your presentation/response. If you've done your job right, you've already established that:

- They need it.

- They can afford it.

- Its value far outweighs its costs.

In other words, the sale is made. But, of course, salespeople know that things are seldom so pat, so we need to know how to handle various types of objections in case we encounter them. We'll address those objections in Chapter 7.

Presentation Tips

Presentation and the close are two parts of one whole. One naturally leads to the other.

☛ *Preparation is the key to a successful presentation.* Know your facts. Write out and memorize the most important phrases that clearly and persuasively express these facts.

For example, there are certain important euphemisms that I employ in my presentation. I never say, "Our insert is in the back of the magazine." Instead, I say, "Our insert with your ad would fall in the 'People' section of the magazine." Or else I say, "Your ad would be placed in one of the most highly read sections of the magazine."

I never refer to *expenditures*, always *investments;* and I always represent the investment in the smallest possible amount, weekly or monthly rather than a lump sum.

Whenever I talk about an advertisement's reach, I don't refer to subscribers but to how many people in the target audience will be reading the company's message—that is, the number of impressions they will be getting. I do this because impressions represent a larger number, so it makes it easier to compare print to broadcast. Now we're talking apples to apples. I also always demonstrate how my product will increase a company's ROI.

Tip: I have found that two things make a big difference in learning to prepare for a presentation: The first is getting the help and advice of a professional sales trainer, coach, or manager. The second is videotaping. Although it can be very difficult, even painful, to watch ourselves, warts and all, with stumblings, bumblings, and twitches, it's amazing how much our strengths can be maximized and our weaknesses minimized when we see ourselves as others see us.

☛ *Know and include as much information as possible about your prospect's company.* For example, knowing what the company's annual sales are shows you've done your homework. Moreover, it shows you also care enough about the prospect and his or her company to have done some research.

It's often easier to obtain corporate information than you might think. Annual reports are there for the asking. Your credit department might have information available about the number of employees, annual sales, and related things. Business publications might contain articles regarding the company's industry. And, of course, you can obtain great information on the Internet from the company's own corporate Web site.

Demonstrating knowledge of their business will always impress top management and significantly enhance your credibility.

☛ *Be relaxed and conversational, not recitational.* There should be a comfortable flow. Use contractions. Use colloquialisms (but not jargon), for example, "awesome," "over-the-top," "outside the box." Where appropriate, use sports references, such as "pass the ball," "hit a home run," "cross the finish line," "slam dunk." These are *visual* and give color to your presentation.

☛ *Spice it up.* Use a dramatic opening, if appropriate. Develop as exciting and as interactive a presentation as possible. Find ways for prospects to participate in your presentations, such as touching the product, smelling the perfume you're offering, testing the new computer your company makes, driving the new car you're showing, virtually visiting the new plant on the Web, doing a side-by-side comparison between your product and the one they've been using—letting them fill in the blanks.

☛ *Create a demonstration to emphasize value.* Here's a demonstration I developed that people tell me they remember years later. My product is a very focused one. It costs the prospect more to reach every customer, but every potential customer we reach is one of the prospect's precious target market. So in order to emphasize value over cost, I literally leave the room at some point during our discussion. From outside the doorway, I explain that many more people can now hear what I'm saying, but only the people in the room are at all interested in what I'm saying. This little bit of theater demonstrates vividly how value lies not in the sheer numbers of people reached but in reaching precisely those that the prospect needs to reach.

This is an example of using a demonstration to emphasize the value of my product. Your product or service will have its own value message. Creating an interesting way to demonstrate it effectively will vastly improve the chances of your message being favorably remembered and, more important, favorably acted upon.

☛ *Keep a one-on-one feeling for group presentations.* If you are presenting to a group, find out ahead of time about each person who will be there. Look at each person in the audience, not your notes. If there is a screen behind you, turn your head occasionally, but keep your body facing the audience. Use your body language to emphasize only important points. And as with any presentation, know your script cold.

☛ *Always give your ideas a positive slant.* Use words such as "more," "better," "best," "accomplish," "goal," and "attain."

Tip: Of course, make sure that all your materials and samples are fresh and easily accessible. Tailor your presentation according to the number and makeup of your audience. A one-on-one presentation requires different equipment, materials, and methods than a presentation to a group.

☛ Most important, *always keep your focus on the close.*

No matter what the prospect says, no matter what you say, no matter what personal conversation or tangents may arise, always remember your responsibility and your mission, which is "to provide a product or service that will change the person's life for the better."

Many people think presentation is everything. And though I agree that a good, polished presentation is important, it's far from being everything or even the most important part of a sale. The way you understand, restate, and respond to the prospect's needs and how he or she processes information is far more important.

The Close—It Almost Just Happens

If you've met all your responsibilities up to this point, you have done the following:

- ☞ You've qualified the prospect.

- ☞ You've related to the prospect.

- ☞ You've understood how the prospect processes information.

- ☞ You've inquired about the prospect's needs.

- ☞ You've presented/responded, and then answered the prospect's initial objections.

- ☞ You've summarized and reviewed the benefits.

It's no longer an "if" situation, it is simply a "when" situation. However, you do *need to ask,* "When?"

chapter 6

recognizing the close—just reconfirm and ask "when"

THIS IS IT! The moment you've been working toward, and now it's finally happening. And make no mistake, even though by following the first four steps, the final half-step almost "just happens" by itself, it's still a very exciting, exhilarating time. In fact, you must make certain that you overcome any knee-jerk reaction that something great is happening for you. Stay focused on how terrific this is going to be for the prospect. He or she should be enthusiastic about what is happening, and you should certainly share that enthusiasm. But remember the following:

☞ Be very casual. (Don't let on how excited you may be.)

☛ Reconfirm the major reasons the *prospect* has stated showing that what you offer is what he or she needs.

☛ Depending on the type of prospect, offer either a date or a
selection of dates for delivery of your product or service. You
might ask: "Would March be a good time to begin?" or
"Would you be ready to begin in March or would April be
better (more feasible, comfortable, etc.)?" You can also simply ask, "When will be the best time for you to begin utilizing our services or product?"

Closing—Advancing the Buying Decision

*I believe a great salesperson has a tremendous commitment to excellence
and a desire to be the best he or she can be. They should have a willingness to do the things unsuccessful people won't do.*

Howard Cowan, President,
Cowan Financial Group

The buying decision is often complex, so you may not get an
agreement to buy on day one. Keeping your focus on the close, you
must establish what the next step is. Do you need to bring in the
newest research? Do you need to bring in a systems analyst? Do you
need to meet with anyone else at the company?

You not only need to establish the "who" and "what" but also the
"where" and especially the *"when."* Think of yourself as a news
reporter writing your opening paragraph. You must establish: who,
what, where, when, why, and how. If you don't get a yes, you must
immediately ask, "What is the next step?" Without this crucial five-
word question, the entire facilitation process comes to a sudden halt
or wanders weakly off course.

Remember, you're asking these questions for *the prospect's* sake as well as your own. Never feel nervous or guilty about asking them.

Savoring the Fruits of Success

Congratulations! You did what you had to do. You've followed the steps: *You had the right attitude; you developed a strong rapport; you inquired constructively; your presentation reflected the prospect's needs; you asked for the order.* You've lived up to your responsibility. You're making people's lives better. You're making money, and you have every right to feel proud and revel in your accomplishment.

Believe it or not, many salespeople neglect this important self-congratulatory step. You need this step not only for a satisfying emotional close to the process itself but also because, by focusing on the positive things you did and the positive reactions you obtained, you are developing valuable ammunition for your future sales.

Next time you'll be able to visualize, as we described in an earlier chapter, and recall the positive feelings, reactions, emotions, and results of this successful episode. Consequently, you'll be better equipped to do your job.

The successful close is not the end of anything, but rather the beginning of the official business relationship with the people in that company. Your prospect has been promoted to client.

Forget about the sales you hope to make and concentrate on the service you want to render. I tell our salespeople that if they would start out each morning with the thought of, "I want to help as many people as possible today," instead of, "I want to make as many sales as possible today," they would find a more easy and open approach to their buyers, and they would make more sales.

—Harry Bullis, former Chairman of the Board, General Mills, courtesy of *Bits and Pieces*, published by Economics Press, Inc.

A successful close is also a great emotional springboard for making your next calls.

Successful Referrals

While you're still basking in the glow of your success, it is the best time to pick up the telephone and call others in a similar category or to make the difficult calls you've been avoiding.

Leverage your success by asking for a referral. Simply ask, "Do you know of anyone personally or professionally who could utilize our services?" There'll never be a better time than this early euphoric stage to ask for a referral. This doesn't mean that after a few months when things are going great that you shouldn't ask the referral question again.

When it comes to asking for referrals, I have found insurance agents to be the undisputed champions. Whether or not you buy from them, they always ask, "Do you know of anyone else I might be of service to?" That's probably why I know so many very successful insurance agents.

Hey! What Went Wrong?

Don't be upset if you don't walk away with a signed contract at the end of the first meeting. You know you have met with key decision-makers and that they are either ready to buy, or you've established what the next step in the buying process is. If there are any obstacles that might arise during this next step, you'll be well prepared to overcome them after you've read Chapter 7.

prospecting and
points to ponder

overcoming obstacles to success

IN A PERFECT world, the buying decision has been made in your favor by this point. In the real world, however, there will often be obstacles you'll encounter before everything is signed, sealed, and delivered.

Be Preemptive

Don't get sand-trapped. Skilled golfers know to avoid hazards on the course. If you just go for the cup and ignore the traps, chances are excellent that you'll end up in one. It makes good sense to do all you reasonably can to avoid them.

If you can anticipate sand traps or obstacles that might be standing in the way of a favorable buying decision, you must address them in advance. You must either play around them or play over them. For example, if you represent a small company competing for business with an industry giant, you might say something like: "I can appreciate how you *feel* about dealing with a small company that's not yet as well known as some others are."

You might explain to the prospect, "Our major clients, like (list biggest names possible), initially *felt* the same way. They have *found*, however, that working with a smaller company like ours has given them much more flexibility, a certain freshness, highly personalized treatment, and a quicker turnaround than they could have gotten with a bigger company."

Tip: Remember the Feel, Felt, Found Method for overcoming an objection. It's simple. Just say, "I understand how you *feel*... others have felt the same way... but they have found that..." With this method, you can often turn a potential negative into a positive.

Sometimes, however, this might not be possible. For example, the Magazine Network that I represent requires a significantly longer lead time than other magazines, newspapers, radio, television, and other media. Based on past painful experiences, I *recognize pre-emptively* that this may be an obstacle. So, I express an *understanding*, appreciation, or empathy with the buyer's concern. Next, I describe how others initially might have *felt* similarly and how, subsequently, they *found* my product more valuable than the competition. I always try to "neutralize the negatives."

Typically, I might say: "In case there's any concern about a longer lead time with Media Networks, I just want to let you know that the marketing directors at other banks, like ABC Savings Bank, also initially expressed a similar concern. Now they're one of our longest-running and most successful clients. They found that our magazines afforded them a unique opportunity (national magazines at local rates in key local markets) to reach their best mortgage prospects."

By shifting the focus from lead time to a "unique opportunity to promote specific value to a finely targeted market," I regularly neutralize a common hazard.

Then there is the infamous price hazard: "Your product sounds too expensive." If we have done our job in establishing the great value of our product or service, this may not be a significant obstacle. However, "price" may still be used by the prospect as a negotiating ploy, or be raised merely out of habit.

To get past this obstacle, first clarify and try to quantify what the buyer means by expensive. You might ask, "Oh, in what way do you feel that it may be too expensive?" And remember: Since you've already established the value of your product or service, now would be a good time to remind the prospect of that value. Point out the value of your product or service relative to other choices the prospect might have.

As I have mentioned, deflate objections by bringing them up yourself. For example, let's say in radio commercial sales you know your station has low ratings, so when you go in to see the customer, you'd say, "Would you rather have ten people in your store who buy or a hundred people who don't buy?"

One of the best examples of focusing on value, as a buying criterion, is one we're all familiar with—the sound system purchase. You have in mind how much you want to spend when you go into the store, and you tell the salesperson your range. He will let you listen to a system in that price range. It sounds really good to you. You say, "Great! I'll take it." He says, "Great. Good choice. But did you know that for just a little more, you could have this?" He then plays the next best system for you. It sounds much better than what you thought you had liked so much just a moment ago. "Wow!" you say. "That's incredible. I'll take that one!" This little step-up scenario continues until you've reached an absolute upper limit. The systems sound so much better at each step for such a small incremental increase in price. Then comes the knockout. As you nervously waver in you final buying decision, starting to perspire from sticker shock, the salesperson says, "Listen again to the system you're considering." You listen. It's the moon and stars. Then he says, "Now, listen to the system you wanted just a few minutes ago." He plays the system you had initially listened to, and it now sounds like tin cans and string. Buying decision made. Value wins out over price.

Whether you're buying a sound system, an air conditioner, a car, or a house, a good salesperson will always stress value. For just a bit more, you'll be buying huge advantages. It's what you're getting for your money, rather than how much you're spending.

I recently questioned my savvy Merrill Lynch investment counselor, Amanda Hinton, about my discomfort with having to pay a 2 percent front-load expense fee on a certain conservative fund she was recommending, versus the standard 1.3 percent fee on most other funds. Instead of becoming defensive, she simply asked, "In hindsight, Carol, would you rather have paid the 0.7 percent fee difference for this conservative fund instead of 1.3 percent for a fund that lost you 50 percent of its value, as most have done in the past two years?" I congratulated her on her point-making skills.

Thus, having removed the objection, you can now ask, "So if (this objection) price were overcome . . . you would buy?" *Tip: Do not discuss price until you have absolutely established value.* When your prospect is focusing heavily on price, it's very tempting to break this rule and meet her head on. Resist. You can't win.

Once you have successfully removed price as an objection by demonstrating the importance of value, you must remind the prospect that there is now nothing standing in the way of buying. Restrain yourself, however, from jumping to, "Okay, that's taken care of, now sign here."

Take a breath. *Review.* Very briefly, take the prospect through all the specific reasons that he has expressed to you (with your guidance), saying why he wants your product. It's important that the prospect always feel that this is something that she wants to do, not simply something that you want her to do.

Repelling the Surprise Attack

Of course, even the most experienced professional can't anticipate every hazard every time. What happens when you are faced with an objection for the first time?

First, let the prospect vent. *Listen* carefully and attentively to what he or she is saying. Don't interrupt! A good thing to do is to take notes. This diffuses your natural urge to interrupt defensively. It also demonstrates that you're taking the prospect's words seriously. Next, *express your empathy* for the prospect's point of view. You may use phrases such as:

- ☛ "I can understand how you feel."

- ☛ "I can appreciate your position."

☛ "You've expressed your position very well."

Then, *clarify* exactly what the prospect means in a concerned, nonemotional, and factual manner. For example, you could ask:

☛ "It seems that this is the situation ... [then *summarize*]. Is that the way you see it?"

☛ "Can you tell me exactly what happened?"

☛ "Can you clarify what took place?"

By removing the emotion, you're again in a position to focus on the facts and, thereby, find a resolution to the buyer's concern. Finding a *solution* may be as simple as finding what the prospect or client wants. You may want to ask the following questions:

"What do you think *we* should do?"

"How do you see this being resolved?"

Or, in coming up with your own solution, you may want to ask:

"Would this be a good idea?"

"Does this idea resolve the issue?"

When one of my larger clients was considering canceling, naturally I wanted to know why. When the client told me that the response did not justify the cost, I thought, "Oh, no ... what can I do to save this account?"

Because I strongly believed that we had the right product, I figured there was something I could do to rescue this account. Since I wasn't in a position to increase response, I had to find a way to efficiently reduce expenditure. So, I suggested that they concentrate their expenditures on the areas of greatest return and eliminate expenditures in more marginal areas. They did.

Your four best weapons for repelling a surprise attack and turning it to your advantage are to:

1. Listen to the prospect vent.

2. Express your empathy.

3. Clarify what the prospect means.

4. Find a solution.

Finding a Solution

Somehow, I can't believe there are many heights that can't be scaled by a man who knows the secret of making dreams come true. This special secret, it seems to me, can be summarized in four Cs. They are: Curiosity, Confidence, Courage, and Constancy. And the greatest of these is Confidence. When you believe a thing, believe it all over, implicitly and unquestioningly.

—Walt Disney, creator of mouse-based entertainment empire

Once we have let the prospect vent, while listening carefully to what he or she has said and clarifying the prospect's concerns by restating them, it may be necessary to creatively improvise a solution, as in the above example.

The keys to improvisation, whether you're talking about acting, music, or negotiating, are creativity and confidence. In order to be creative, you must be a master of your craft and have had a range of practical experiences from which to draw. To gain confidence, you must believe that there is a solution for virtually any problem and that *you can find it*. There's never a dead end. This can-do attitude can become a self-fulfilling prophecy.

At age 25, Lance Armstrong was one of the world's best cyclists. He proved it by winning the World Championship, the Tour Du Pont, and multiple Tour de France races. Lance Armstrong seemed invincible, and the future ahead was bright indeed.

Then, doctors told him he had cancer.

Next to the challenge he now faced, bike racing seemed insignificant. The diagnosis was testicular cancer, the most common cancer in men age 15 to 35. If detected early, its cure rate is a promising 90 percent. Like most young, healthy men, Armstrong ignored the warning signs and never imagined the seriousness of his condition.

Having gone untreated, the cancer had spread to Lance's abdomen, lungs, and brain.

At this point, a combination of physical conditioning, a strong support system, and his competitive spirit took over.

Armstrong declared himself not a cancer victim but a cancer survivor. He took an active role in educating himself about his disease and its treatment. Armed with knowledge and confidence in medicine, he underwent aggressive treatment and beat the disease.

Armstrong defeated cancer as he defeated his competitors, by absolutely refusing to accept anything less than winning.

Throughout history, those who believed in themselves and their ideas gained the great victories. They were not daunted by criticism, cynicism, nay-saying, or ridicule. Generals know this. Coaches know this. You know it, too. Remember it. Use it. Be a champion.

Getting "Yes"-ed to Death

Now we come to an especially insidious trap: the kindly "yes."

Ironically, the villains who set this trap are usually the friendly, open types, the Al Roker Type. (Remember?) The "yessers" just won't say no. They want you to like them, and they feel that turning you down won't make that happen. So, instead of simply telling you no— and hopefully expressing their objections so that you can either respond or move on—yessers make you feel that you're on track . . . that they're only "this far" from signing a contract . . . that you can relax and count your commissions. Then BAM! No buy. All you can do is stammer, "But I thought . . . but, didn't you say yesterday that . . ." and other what-the-hell-just-happened phrases. Reality rushes in. You've been yessed to death.

Here's a surefire way to avoid it, especially when you're dealing with The Al Roker Type. Get specific answers to specific questions. Do it in a friendly, professional manner, of course, but make certain you do it. Get answers to the who, what, when, where, why, and how questions, so that you will be able to protect yourself from the deadly yessers. Or, you may have to review the benefits that you have agreed upon and ask, "What am I missing?"

After all, it is your *responsibility* to help the prospect.

Obstacles Recap

In meeting objections or overcoming obstacles, don't sweat the small stuff. Don't even address token resistance. After all, everyone likes to feel as if he or she is in control. Let your prospects feel that way.

Remember, don't be confrontational. Be a reassurer and a problem-solver.

The steps are simple: *Listen, show empathy, clarify the problem, and find a solution.*

The most effective salespeople? They get close to the client by asking the right questions, getting to know the business, and then delivering within that context. While knowing what they're selling and whom they're selling to is important, delivery is critical. When there's a good idea, whether it sprouted from my organization or from the sales side, I have to believe that the salespeople can make it happen. That is, they must be empowered to work with the client in a true CRM (customer relationship management) environment. I surely don't want to be encumbered with the bureaucracies of their organization. Delivery should be seamless. When it is, doing business is a pleasure.

—Dorothy Durkin, Associate Dean, Office of Public Affairs and Student Services, NYU School of Continuing Education and Professional Studies

prospecting

EXCEPT FOR THOSE rare or nonexistent times when you simply get lucky or have a relative in the business or when you have received a referral, prospecting is always the first step toward success.

Pretend the year is 1849, and you're in California. You know there is gold in "them thar" hills. All you have to do is find it and take it away.

Preparation

You can't mine for gold using only a teaspoon. You need the right tools. As a salesperson, your most important tool would be a well-crafted, well-thought-out, well-rehearsed script.

A script does not imply a canned speech or word-for-word recitation. Rather, it is a comprehensive outline of the information you need to get an appointment, and nothing more. To prepare the best possible script, you should use the help of a sales coach or manager. Armed with a great script, your call/appointment ratio will be much higher, your confidence will grow, and you'll be more successful.

Getting Through the Screen

Get a name to ask for. To do so, you can call beforehand and find out the right person. Then hang up and call back.

Ask for the prospect by name, as if you know the person, without using "mister" or "missus." I often ask for the prospect by first name only. It does work. Try it. Then identify yourself and give your company name (you'll be asked for it anyway). If the person is not available, find out when he or she will be back in the office and call back then, without leaving your number.

View the screener as a helper. The screener wants to help his or her boss speak to the right people. So make sure you let the screener know you're one of the people the boss should speak with. Make screeners feel important, because they are. Whenever possible, try to call back rather than leaving your name and number. Most prospects don't return cold calls. That's a fact. So, by not leaving your name and number, you're not leaving yourself open for rejection or being thought of as a pest.

Whenever possible, try to glean as many informational tidbits from the screener as possible. For example, if the screener says that the boss is on vacation, find out, if possible, where he or she went. Use your tidbits when you speak with the prospect. It will help break the ice and possibly score you some first impression points.

Organizing Your Prospecting Efforts

If you are living up to your *responsibility*, you'll be making a lot of calls. Every call will have its own set of related details, such as when the person will be available, the name of the assistant, the competitive background of the industry, the factoids you've gleaned, et cetera.

In the so-called old days, a good salesperson's most valuable possessions were his or her 3- by 5-inch cards and a desk diary/calendar. Or, if you were like me, you'd have had piles of paper scraps, Post-it Notes®, and newspaper articles on your desk. I wasted many hours each week, hunting for the right scrap in the right pile. Just keeping organized was practically a full-time job.

Computers and database management have changed all that. Now, you can organize as you work. It's easy and, for me, fun. No more scraps of paper, no more forgetting to call someone, and no more looking for the name of the assistant. (Well, almost never.) Now you have everything in one place and even an alarm to remind you when to call. Without a computer and database management software, you're operating in the Dark Ages.

These software programs also have a simplified word-processing system that helps you to compose letters, pull up the address on the letter itself, print or fax the letter, and file it—all in a few minutes.

These database management systems also keep track of your appointments, tell you when to make telephone calls, and even make them for you. These systems keep a record of all telephone calls for instant retrieval. This information can be printed out as a contact report to eliminate writing out call reports, which is not a favorite activity of salespeople. These systems are designed to be user friendly. You can be up and running in an amazingly short period of time.

As a part of keeping yourself healthy and avoiding neck problems caused by cradling your telephone, I highly recommend using a headset. A headset also gives you more mobility and allows you greater efficiency.

IDENTIFY YOUR BEST PROSPECTS

Ask yourself, "Who could best benefit from what I have to offer?" Before you try to sell refrigerators to Eskimos, go after those who would benefit most from refrigeration instead.

It's amazing how many salespeople include the metaphorical Eskimos in with their prime prospects. To them, "a prospect is a prospect is a prospect." This is a dangerous trap. Besides being able to benefit from what you offer, your prospect *must also be able to afford* what you're offering. Your time is too valuable to waste it on prospects that can't buy. Even though it might feed your ego to talk to *someone you know* will be excited about your offer, you won't be feeding yourself or your family.

You must do everything you can to qualify a prospect. Check with Dun and Bradstreet. Find out what they're doing now. Consider seasonality in your call planning. Know if they have a budget, et cetera.

WORK ON YOUR "SNIFFER"

I have developed my own sensitive "sniffer" to find new business opportunities. Essentially, this involves digging around for clues to potential accounts. I fine-tune the "sniffer" by reading the trades to see what is hot. The local newspaper's business section also helps me to sniff out new advertisers or businesses that can use my help.

I also go through tear sheets (final printed ads) from our own publications to find emerging categories that have the greatest number of accounts represented. I also try to find patterns based on accounts my agencies call to discuss. In addition, I look at the editorial calendars to see what special issues we have coming up.

Sharing insights with my colleagues is also key. With constant training, my "sniffer" has become very sensitive and accurate. Yours can, too.

Getting the Appointment

When you have the prospect on the line, first, whenever possible, mention a referral name, as in "John Jones suggested I call you." Next, identify yourself and your company. Try not to give your name first, especially if you are leaving a voice message, so you can avoid being deleted before leaving your message. Another strategy is to mention the success you've had with other companies in a similar field. Then add, "I have some ideas I'd like to share with you on how your company can benefit from what we do." Finally, ask for a choice of which day and time during the following week would be most convenient.

Often you will be interrupted with challenging questions, which you should field in a confident, professional, and nonconfrontational manner. After all, it's your responsibility to help make this person's life better; and it begins with getting an appointment. That's your goal. Don't be sidetracked by selling your services on the telephone. That's for telemarketers—and that's another book. You need to initially meet someone face-to-face to develop rapport and to know how this person processes information.

SAMPLE SCRIPT

"Good morning, Mr. Brown."

"Jerry Johnson suggested that I call because we've just completed working with Acme Imaging on a very successful program that increased their patient responses by more than 25 percent."

"I'd like to meet with you to discuss how we can be successful for you, too."

"My name is Harry Smith, and I am with Medical Innovations, a division of XYZ International."

"Would next week be convenient for you? Or the week after?"

A great salesperson is a powerfully self-motivated person; someone who makes things happen—not waits for them to happen. My personal mantra is ten two-letter words: If it is to be, it is up to me.

—Jim Smith, President, Jim Smith Chevrolet

chapter 9

everybody hates making cold calls

BEGINNING IN childhood, we learned that there were certain things in life we considered unpleasant that were nevertheless necessary, such as brushing our teeth, eating our vegetables, doing our homework, cleaning our room, going to the dentist, or kissing Aunt Emily. You learned that performing these seemingly unpleasant tasks *faithfully* would eventually result in a positive outcome.

For most people, cold calling falls firmly into this unpleasant, but necessary category. Cold calling must be approached with the same discipline that you used successfully in other areas of your life, such as learning to play a sport or an instrument or establishing good study habits.

Harness the tremendous negative energy generated by your fears and turn it to your positive advantage.

You know the signs all too well. The cold sweaty palms and forehead, the shaky hands, the knot in your stomach, the choked voice. These are the signs of fear. Everyone experiences fear. I look at it as evidence that I care about something. After all, if I am unconcerned about the outcome of an undertaking, I must have no feelings at all toward it.

Good salespeople or performers of any kind who "put themselves out there" use this caring component to connect with people. When you face your fears and perform in spite of them, your message projects as being passionate. "This is important to me," it says. That means a lot to whomever you're communicating with. The person will understand at a very deep level that you're sincerely trying to do something for him or her. It shows in your voice. It shows in your body language.

You may not have thought of fear as a tool before. In fact, it's one of your most effective ones. Challenge yourself and learn how to use it.

Fear Is a Tool, But Desperation Is Deadly

If a prospect feels you're desperate for a sale, you've lost him or her. Period. Desperation means that you're focused on your achievement rather than on the prospect's needs. As Deborah Rosado Shaw says in her book *Dream Big*, "Desperation is deadly. People can smell it and they run from it."

If you become scared or discouraged while making cold calls, think about the following scenario:

Gena Harper is a downhill skier, windsurfer, and rock climber. She became the top-producing vice president for investments at Morgan Stanley Dean Witter at the age of thirty-three. She is almost completely blind.

Kind of puts your discouragement in its place, doesn't it?

The art of being wise is the art of knowing what to overlook.
— William James, American psychologist and philosopher

The Process of Cold Calling

☞ *Define your goal.* How many new appointments do you need each week to be successful? How many calls do you need to make to secure those new appointments? The rule of thumb is that for every twenty calls you make, you'll get at least one appointment.

In this context, the definition of a call is a successfully completed dial. That means wrong numbers don't count, but voice mail does— even though you may not want to leave a message. More on this a little later in this chapter.

Organize your list. Begin by selecting prospects who hold the promise of the greatest financial return, those who have the greatest potential to be one of the 20 percent of your customers who are responsible for 80 percent of your business. I call them members of my 80/20 Club.

Some prospects will be more accessible than others because of their position, such as purchasing agent or marketing director. Others may be more difficult to reach, because of their travel schedules or their "gatekeepers." You can go back and forth between the ones who are more and the ones who are less accessible to keep cold calling more interesting.

Give your potential 80/20 Club members a special place in your database. They are your prime prospects.

Next, go to the prospects you find who have a high potential and are fairly accessible. By that, I mean these people are similar to purchasing agents or marketing people who are more likely to see you. Put these on another sheet, in another colored file folder, or in another section of your database. These would also be prime prospects.

Then, go to the prospects where the timing is most propitious. By that, I mean that there is seasonality involved, a special offer involved, or you know they are in the midst of budget planning. Put these on another sheet in another colored file folder, or in another section of your database.

You also may want to organize your prospects by category and then do a category blitz of calls and appointments. The benefit of category calling is that you may get information on one call that you can use on another. It's also easier to organize the materials you would be carrying on those calls.

Also, create a folder for the less likely prospects. When times are slow, it's always comforting to know that you have a good bank of prospects.

I personally find it more interesting—and, frankly, less daunting—to move between categories in making my calls. It gives me more of a feeling of choice in the matter.

In defining my cold-call goals for the day, I make sure that I call and try to get through to at least three to ten of my prime prospects. The number will vary based on how many appointments I have that day.

I also like to use the 10-10-10 System, which refers to ten new calls, ten existing contact calls, and ten follow-up calls.

☛ *Know when to call.* Naturally, the answer would be anytime and all the time. However, for you, there will be an optimum time of the day to call.

What is your highest energy time? Are you an early bird? Or does it take you a while to get cranked up?

Try to concentrate your calls during the time that coincides with your highest energy level and the likelihood of not being in meetings. I have found that calling right before lunch and sometimes right after are good times to find people in their offices so you can set an appointment. Often, the higher-level decision-makers are in their offices either very early and/or very late. Force yourself to call at *their* optimum time, even if it is not necessarily yours.

Try not to schedule appointments or take calls during your optimum cold-calling time. Cold calling is like gardening. You must prepare the ground, tend the weeds, fertilize, and add new seeds or new plants to have a successful garden. If you simply let nature take its course, your garden probably won't succeed. You need to devote the necessary time and discipline to succeed in either endeavor.

As with a musician or an athlete, natural talent is not enough to ensure success. You must have the discipline to practice, analyze, learn, and grow.

In sales, being charming, attractive, and bright are natural benefits; but without discipline, they're not enough.

☛ *The Calling Game: keeping score.* One of the basic tenets of child psychology is to make unpleasant tasks palatable by turning them into a game. Remember, getting a sticky star for each library book you read during the summer (for those of you who are old enough to remember summer reading programs)? Or maybe you remember passing the time on long family trips by keeping track of license plates?

Using the same psychology helps me to maintain the discipline I need to be a successful cold caller or prospector.

Here's how I play my "Calling Game":

On a sheet of paper, I make a simple hatch mark for every number I dial.

$$8{:}30 \text{ a.m. } / / / \overset{s}{\cancel{0}} / / \overset{s}{\cancel{0}} / / / \overset{s}{\cancel{0}} / \text{ } 11{:}30 \text{ a.m.}$$

If I reach the person, I put an S over the hatch mark to indicate that I've spoken to him or her. When I make an appointment, I circle the hatch mark. I also write down the time when I make my first and last dial to see how well I've done in terms of keeping my word to myself and reinforcing my self-image as a responsible person. This also provides me with an ongoing scorecard.

Some tips for improving your score:

☞ Don't set yourself up for defeat by setting unrealistically high goals.

☞ Keep track of the time you made the calls so you can zero in on when the prospect is mostly likely to be available. You can also compete against yourself and see which day you were able to complete your calls in a shorter period of time.

☛ Try not to leave a voice mail message unless absolutely necessary. Instead, dial "0" and ask for someone who would know when would be the best time to reach the prospect, using the prospect's first and last name. Remember, you should sound like you know the prospect and are just checking for the most convenient time to call back. As mentioned previously, refer to the prospect by his or her first name when making inquiries.

☛ When you make the appointment, be sure to ask if anyone else will be in the meeting with you.

☛ Keep the game interesting for yourself by using the 10-10-10 System described earlier, and keep your goals realistic.

☛ Keep focused by trying not to take or return calls during the "game."

☛ When you make an appointment, immediately enter the prospect's name in your database or PDA. This serves as a reward mechanism in the Pavlovian manner.

☛ Track your calling volume for the week each Friday, and analyze what obstacles prevented you from making more calls.

☛ Congratulate yourself, and then give yourself a treat if you met your calling goals for the entire week.

Telephone Attitude

Here are some suggestions that can help you feel better and perform better when you are "working the phones."

CLOSE YOUR EYES AND VISUALIZE

Closing my eyes and visualizing success before each phone call, I imagine the call going well and focus on a positive outcome.

DO IT WITH MIRRORS

I always have a mirror on my desk to help me remember to smile. I always try to be aware, by their language, whether the person on the other end is a visual, auditory, or kinesthetic. I can then identify, mirror, and present to them in their style.

SIT UP . . . STAND UP . . . BE UP

By simply sitting up straight, I put myself in an "up" mode—no matter what transpired on the previous call.

If you don't agree that physiology affects psychology, try this idea from top sales trainer Tony Robbins: "Slouch over and notice how you feel (particularly in your stomach). Now sit up straight with your shoulders back, looking forward. How do you feel now? Ready to take on the world?"

When I have the client on the telephone, I stand up to keep my posture and voice in a presentation mode. Standing up helps me to concentrate.

You might also want to have a cassette playing your favorite uplifting music. You can have it playing softly in the background or just turn it on between calls.

No one can make you feel inferior without your consent.

—Eleanor Roosevelt

THE 1 PERCENT SOLUTION

Anything worth doing is worth doing better, especially when you spend so much of your life doing it. With this in mind, I make a conscious effort to improve my on-phone performance by a guesstimated 1 percent with each call. If successful, that means that I'm a much better prospector at the end of each week than I was at the beginning. The 1 percent solution is a small incremental investment that pays big dividends. Try it. Put a sticky note that says "1 percent better" on your mirror to remind you.

NEW GOALS

Every Friday, Sunday, or Monday, depending on which day you prefer, write out your goals for the week based on your appointment schedule.

WHERE DO PROSPECTS COME FROM?

Prospects are made, not born. I consider every advertisement, news story, trade article, personnel change, introduction, and chance meeting to be a potential lead.

> While waiting interminably in the self-service line of a restaurant, I struck up a casual conversation with the young woman behind me. I discovered that she was a media supervisor for a large media-buying service. She subsequently became one of my clients.

Don't be afraid to call on a long shot or a hunch. These forays can lead to some of your biggest successes.

> We love pianos. My mother plays. My husband plays. I listen. And, in fact, my mother gave us a beautiful Yamaha upright

for our apartment as a wedding present. Through some very good luck and smart bidding, we were able to acquire a brand-new Yamaha Disklavier at a charity auction. This is a full-size acoustic piano that plays computer disks recorded by some of the world's greatest performers, precisely duplicating the pressure on every key and pedal! It's like having the world's best players in your own living room. It even allows you to record your own great piano performances. So, we are able to have my mother's music in our home, even when she is not with us. We thought that it was the greatest purchase we had ever made. We were thrilled. The Disklavier became a very important part of our lives.

A few weeks after it was delivered, I noticed a Disklavier advertisement in a national magazine. I showed it to my husband. We were appalled. The advertisement failed to convey the wonder of the instrument, such as the magic of bringing a live performance into your home. We agreed that my husband should call the company the next day and express his dismay—and his concepts for a proper positioning.

He called. When he reached the marketing director, he said, "I hope this won't bruise any feelings, but I'm a piano lover, a piano player, a Disklavier owner, and an ad man. All four of us feel that your present ad completely neglects the great power of the product." Incredibly, the marketing director laughed and said, "I just came out of a meeting filled with a roomful of Yamaha executives who very much agree with you. How would you do it?"

The answers apparently satisfied him because the Yamaha Keyboard Division became a valued client of my husband's company. Also, the marketing director became one of our closest friends.

REFERRALS—WARMING UP COLD CALLING

In a perfect world, cold calling would be unnecessary. All your leads would be referrals. You'd have a connection (a name), a telephone number, and a success story to get you in the door.

So, to make your world as "perfect" as possible, get as many referrals as possible. It's as simple as asking, "So, do you know of anyone who might benefit from our product or service?" You might be surprised at how willingly people will give you this information.

Referrals come from the following three basic sources:

1. Your client base

2. Your family, friends, acquaintances, and business associates

3. Those who can't use your services, but may know someone who might

With your client base, keep track in your computer or on your weekly call sheets for management of when you last asked for a referral. Once every three to six months, call up or invite your client to lunch and ask, "By the way, have you thought of anyone else who might benefit from our services?" Don't make a big deal out of asking for a referral. Just do it during the course of conversation.

Be sure to keep your clients informed of the outcome of their referral and be sure to express your thanks. You may want to do that in a tangible manner.

Asking family and friends for referrals is the easiest. Just fit it in to an appropriate conversation. (This excludes weddings and funerals.)

The third group, those who for whatever reason couldn't use your services, might still be happy to suggest others who might benefit from your product or service. Remember, this includes people whom you may have cold called, as well as presented to.

LEAVING YOU WITH A NUGGET

The qualities of a successful business prospector are similar to those of a successful gold prospector, and include the following:

- The right tools

- Preparation and organization

- Skills to know the difference between fool's gold and real gold

- Determination not to be deterred by temporary setbacks

- Discipline to prospect daily

- Spirit of adventure and wanting to conquer the unknown

Be a successful prospector; cultivate these qualities. Bring home the gold.

The most important quality for sales success is ambition, a driving desire to be successful and to use sales success as the vehicle to accomplish everything else a person wants in their material life. Closely tied to ambition are the qualities of desire, discipline, determination, and decisiveness. If a salesperson has these qualities in sufficient quantity, all of which can be developed with practice, he or she will be successful in any market.

—Brian Tracy, author of *Victory!, Focal Point,* and *TurboStrategy*

ı

learning super's secrets of sales tool maintenance

ONE OF THE most difficult tasks in sales is staying motivated.

You will not always feel physically, mentally, or emotionally at the top of your game. At those times when I'm not physically tip-top, I first congratulate myself for showing up (which some people say is 90 percent of the game anyway). I begin the day with the gentlest tasks such as getting out a prospect mailing or some other noncreative endeavor. I reset my daily goals to an easier-than-usual attainment level and allow myself to rejoice in surpassing them.

Keeping Yourself Healthy

I cannot overemphasize the importance to success of keeping yourself in the best possible physical condition. I read an article in 1995, on the front page of *The New York Times,* debunking the myth that eating a lot of carbohydrates was healthy. It said that 25 percent of the U.S. population is insulin resistant to carbohydrates, resulting in increased hunger, food cravings, and weight gain. I had felt that since embarking on eating more carbohydrates, I was feeling sluggish and also gaining weight. Suspecting that I could be one of the 25 percent who are insulin resistant, I went to the doctor mentioned in the article for a diet that would be filling but not fattening. I was encouraged by my weight loss and subsequently added more exercise: stretching, lifting, and a walking regimen that includes at least three miles a day, five days a week. Tony Robbins talks about undergoing the metamorphosis from fat kid to the slim healthy person he is today as one of the major factors of his success.

If I find that I'm mentally preoccupied by one of the myriad other considerations of my life, I meditate and go to my own special place to focus. I also make sure that I go over my mission statement.

An emotional downer is the most difficult to handle. Your child is sick. Your roof is leaking. The competition beat you out on a major client. Your biggest competitor for the top spot in the company just scored a huge hit. The production department screwed up the postcard insert for your biggest client. You're feeling lower than a catfish looking for bottom food. How do you snap out of it?

Again, I go to my special place and meditate. I see myself as being successful and getting everything I want. I call on my support network for encouragement. (My husband is my number one support person. I also might call a friendly colleague.) I look to magazines, books, or tapes about sales for inspiration.

Finally, I just push myself to begin. I tell myself that the first pre-set amount of time will be spent on just getting going. Once I get into the rhythm of the work, the haze begins to lift, the clouds part, the sun appears, and I'm back on track.

Always look for new, fun, creative ways to stand out from the sales crowd and to keep things interesting for yourself, your clients, and your prospective clients. For example, have your photograph put on your business card, if appropriate. Send a Magic 8-Ball toy ("Improve Your Outlook. Call me.") or chattering teeth toy ("Everybody's Talking About Us") to prospective clients. You could send a light bulb ("For a Brilliant Idea"), an alarm clock ("Time Is Ticking Away"), a shoe in a box ("Now That I Have a Foot in the Door"), or fishing fly ("What Can I Do to Lure You?"). If the person is a golfer and has loads of potential, you could send a nice golf club ("I'd Like to Take a Swing at Your Business").

Imagination is more important than knowledge.

—Albert Einstein

One of the benefits of my liberal arts mindset is that I simply can't get enough information! I enjoy learning from books, magazines, television, corporate meetings, and conversations. I strive to know more about virtually everything! When I come across some tidbit that I think might be of value to a friend, relative, or business associate, I've learned not to assume that they already know it—I share it. This simple gesture is usually appreciated far beyond the effort it took to make it. The more you know, the more you grow.

Read professional publications; take courses. (When I was working at the 3M Company, forty hours of professional training a year was mandatory.) Stay sharp, finely tuned, and well oiled. Join professional organizations and/or trade groups. You will not only learn more but also network and gain referrals that will make your job much easier. Although it might sometimes seem otherwise, these activities are usually an excellent investment of your time.

As with every profession, it is essential to constantly add to your knowledge, to upgrade your skills, and to take advantage of the latest technology. In other words, you should always be learning. Good salespeople need a strong ego and confidence in their abilities. But keep in mind that a know-it-all attitude is supremely counterproductive.

The fact that I am always striving to gain new knowledge, insights, angles, and techniques is, I believe, one of the most important reasons for my success.

Integrity is an indispensable ingredient for success. Your professional integrity may be tested on a daily basis. The temptations are there, such as getting someone to buy something beyond their needs, bringing out a product before it's ready, making a promise you know you can't keep, or stealing an account from an associate. Just a friendly reminder that when you lose your integrity, you lose everything. As many top executives have recently discovered with disastrous results, giving in to quick-money temptations will always come back to haunt you.

Having integrity also makes you want to do more and offer more value to your customers. Insuring that your customers get their money's worth brings you a disproportionate return of professional satisfaction.

Long-term professional selling is less about the level of your skill than the content of your character. True professionals know that skill may help you close the first sale, but integrity keeps customers coming back.
—Ron Tartarella, in *Selling Power*

Conclusion

So, do you feel it? Do you sense it? You're stronger and better. You have a new point of view. You're not a desperate bell-ringing, phone-calling intruder. You're a facilitator—and a professional. You know how to help improve the lives of all those you serve with the benefits of what you have to offer. And, by doing so, you're going to be more successful than ever before possible; and therefore your life will be much happier, too.

If you don't think this book has done that for you, read it again. You missed something. There's real power here. It's worked for me and it *will* work for you.

Now, you know my secrets.

A great salesperson is: passionately energetic, creative and focused on a results-driven solution that best meets their clients' objectives.

—Wayne Powers, President of Media Networks, Inc., AOL/Time Warner

lagniappe

LAGNIAPPE is a Cajun word that means "something extra."

Persistence

Even if you're a perfect and responsible professional—and even if you have faithfully followed every suggestion in this book—there is usually another quality that you need to possess in great measure: persistence.

On handling rejection: Michael Jordan was cut from his high school basketball team.

Many prospects need to be gently, but constantly, reminded that you are there to make their lives better. This can be accomplished either by meeting with them or by continuing discussions previously begun.

Whether you use an old-fashioned diary or a state-of-the-art hi-tech computer management program, staying in touch at a pace dictated by the prospect is essential. You must learn the fine line between being persistent and being a pest. If a mistake is made in this matter, however, make it on the "pest" side and not the "let it slide" side. Often, when you least expect it, your prospect's stars will line up right and they will realize that it's time to ask for your help.

Harlan Sanders was a retired 65-year-old government worker with a chicken recipe. Armed only with that recipe and persistence, he set out to get restaurants to serve his chicken. Nobody was interested in his chicken—not the tenth restaurant, not the one-hundredth restaurant, not the one thousandth restaurant, and not even the two thousandth restaurant! Sanders persisted. The 2,315th restaurant he visited with his chicken said they'd give it a try. That was the beginning of Colonel Sanders and his Kentucky Fried Chicken empire. Colonel Sanders evidently believed in his recipe and in Winston Churchill's philosophy that one should: "Never give in. Never give in. Never . . . never . . . never . . . never."

Our greatest weakness lies in giving up. The most certain way to succeed is to always try just one more time.

—Thomas Edison

Follow-Through

Neglect follow-through and you're dead.

As a responsible salesperson, you absolutely must ensure that you have indeed made life better for your client. If the person who has now put his or her trust in you and your product or service feels seduced and abandoned, they're infinitely less likely to buy from you again.

If there is a problem, you *must* be there to solve it. If there is success, you must be there to share the glory with your client. You've successfully launched a relationship. Nurture it or it will wither.

Every morning, while I'm planning my calls for the day, I think of my current clients first and my prospects second. After all, a happy client is my best sales ammunition.

Live Healthy—Be Healthy—Be Successful

You owe it to yourself, those who care about you, and those you are trying to help with your product or service to be the best you can be. That includes being as *healthy* as you can be.

Do all that you possibly can within the bounds of reality, your personal beliefs, and lifestyle to get and stay physically and mentally at your peak. People are attracted to vitality and distracted by frailty. I apologize if this seems obvious, but it's an important secret of my success—and that is what this book is about.

Financial Responsibility

As with physical health, fiscal health is also essential to success. I try to save a minimum of 15 to 20 percent of my income. My goal is to be able to say to my clients and my company, "I'm for you, but I don't need you."

Some Confidence-Building Props

I keep myself surrounded with mementoes of my successes, such as my degrees, awards, success stories, and letters of congratulations. These are constant reminders that I am a proven achiever and have nothing to fear.

Your Support Team

You can't make it without them, so let them know it!

Surround yourself with people who are positive, caring, and competent. Then always show that you are positive and caring toward them as well.

If you're lucky, your parents are a major part of your support team. When you correctly choose your friends and spouse, they are, too. If not, change them.

Several years ago, I took a Life Design course that put me together with some of the top businesswomen in New York City. The course included defining our goals and using the support of our team members to reach those goals. I met every three to four weeks with the women on my team, and this book was a major result of that course and those meetings. If you're interested in contacting Life Design, contact Gail Blanke at GBLD97@aol.com.

You must learn from the mistakes of others. You can't possibly live long enough to make all of them yourself.

—Sam Levenson, author and humorist

Work hard, play hard, and combine them when you can.

Networking

My managers tell me that I'm really great at this skill. I belong to trade associations. I attend meetings. I accept positions of responsibility. I put together people who have similar interests. I push myself, and it consistently pays off.

I understand very well that networking is difficult for many people because it's difficult for me, too. An innate fear exists of meeting new people. It is the fear of rejection in new situations that goes all the way back to childhood. However, as is the case with most fear situations, you'll find that confronting it head on overcomes it. Be brave and push yourself out there.

Great salespeople like being with people and show it. When entering a room, they don't wait for people to come up to them; they enthusiastically meet and greet.

As a natural and intelligent "people person," breaking the ice should be easy for you. Just take into consideration the setting and circumstances and ask "soft" questions that relate. Include some that don't require just one-word answers. "What have you heard about this speaker?" "How do you think they get such a great turnout?" "Where did you get that incredible tie (or piece of jewelry)?" "What does your company do?" How do you feel about . . . ?" "When was the last time you were here?" Open-ended questions like these will get a conversation going and take the pressure off of you about what to say. You'll be listening more, and as we know, that's what a great salesperson does.

My experience shows that others will appreciate your willingness to break the ice for them and you will reap the benefits of your courage in dollars and cents. Networking can be like running into the surf on a hot day. The water may feel very cold at first. But after a short time, you become accustomed to it and don't want to get out.

Playing the Corporate Game—Remember Whose Football It Is

Remember, as a kid, when you had to play football with someone you did not like because you were playing with his or her football?

To many bright, self-confident, motivated people, the maze of big corporate "stuff" often seems foolish, inefficient, and demoralizing. That is a shame. The reality is that to succeed in a large (or not so large) corporation, you must realize "whose football it is" and learn to play within their rules or go home. (Change companies or start your own.)

Swallow hard, take a deep breath, and willingly do the memos, meetings, and "team" things that are part of the chain of command. And let your maverick tendencies show themselves in creative and constructive ways. Remember you can still be you. It's really just a matter of following some rules along the way.

For Women Only

It's getting better all the time, but it's definitely still there: the "Woman" Thing. If you're female, see yourself as a person first and a woman second. A percentage of others, however, are always going to see you as a woman first (and maybe *only*) and they'll have their big bag of automatic responses.

My advice when dealing with those people is to use it to your advantage. For example, Charlotte Beers was president of one of the world's most successful advertising agencies, Ogilvy & Mather. Shelly Lazarus is chairperson of the agency. Together, they were responsible for bringing the company back from a troubled and declining state to a dynamic and powerful position as a primary force in the industry.

In addition to being extremely bright, talented women and successfully turning the agency around, they have something else in common: the way they succeeded. They both made the best use of their brains, talent, and experience by harnessing the power of their femininity. They didn't use bullying, overly powerful, in-your-face male-type tactics that many women feel they must affect in order to accomplish their goals. Instead, Beers and Lazarus used their natural charm, instincts, and intellect to put together the vision, the team, and the necessary creative incentives to breathe new life into an ailing IBM Corporation.

Anne White was the president of White, Good Advertising—a successful Pennsylvania firm. In the early 1980s, when it was still very difficult for a woman to compete on a high level in a man's world, she showed me that by being hospitable, gracious, and charming, a woman could accomplish things that many other people who did not naturally possess these qualities could not. Anne made it possible for me to see that I could relax, be my feminine self, and excel in the business world.

There is nothing like a dame.

—Irving Berlin

A great salesperson . . .

- ☞ *Doesn't view [himself/herself] as a salesperson. They see themselves as problem solvers and a potential resource for their clients.*

- ☞ *Is curious by nature, which enables them to ask meaningful questions that can ultimately help them in making a sale.*

- ☞ *Is self-motivated and entrepreneurial.*

- ☞ *Thrives on competition.*

- ☞ *Is persuasive.*

☛ *Is fearless.*

☛ *Is a bit insecure . . . always thinking that someone out there is doing more to make the sale than they are.*

☛ *Is willing to go above and beyond a client's expectations. Sales is such a competitive field that they need to stand out from the crowd.*

☛ *Is most importantly . . . honorable and trusted. Their word means something and they will always stand by what they promised.*

At the end of the day, people buy from people, not machines. If all things are equal in a client's mind, the person who gets the sale is the person that they like, trust, and want to do business with.

—Nora McAniff, Executive Vice President, Time Inc.

index

Aaron, Hank, 32
Allen, Woody, 9
Al Roker Type, 62–79, 137
Armstrong, Lance, 136–137
appointments, scheduling, 143,
    151
attitude, 15–19
    importance of positive, 15–16,
        120, 152–155
    mantra of self-affirmation, 17
    mood toys, 18–19
    overcoming negative, 18
    rituals, 18–19
    for telephone calls, 152–155
auditory processing, 47–51
Azar, Brian, 46, 60

background questions, 13–14,
    88–89
Beers, Charlotte, 170
belief in product, 11–12
benefits questions, 105–106
Benjou, Paul, 44
Benson, Herbert, 21
Berlin, Irving, 171
Berra, Yogi, 42
be yourself, 53–54

body language, 56–57
Brown, Chad, 54
Buddha, 15
budget determination, 101
Bullis, Harry, 125
Burns, Robert, 22
Bush, George W., 61

Cabot, Tracy, 45–46
Cahn, Erna, 30
Calling Game, 149–151
caution signal, 115–116
celebrating success, 125–126
chauvinism, 40–41
Cheney, Dick, 61
Chopra, Deepak, 20–21
Churchill, Winston, 28, 35–36
clarifying, 134
Clinton, Bill, 61, 81–82
close, 123–126
    advancing buying decision
        through, 124–125
    focus on, in presentation, 120
    obstacles to, 126, 129–138
    referrals and, 126, 155
    self-congratulation, 125–126
    timing of, 121

clothing, 43, 82
cold calls, 145–157
    fear as tool in, 146–147
    process of making, 147–151
commitment, 27–28
common ground, 44
communication
    body language in, 56–57
    listening in, 41–42, 53,
        133–134, 135
    mirroring in, 44–46
    nonverbal, 56–57
    perspective-taking and, 35–36
    relating in, 39–42
competition, 82
competitors, 14
confidence, 12–14, 168
control, 15–16, 43, 81–82
"cool" people, 60–61
Cowan, Howard, 124
credibility, 11–12

database management systems,
        141–142, 151, 166
decision-making, 101–103
    close in, 124–125
    determining decision-maker,
        101–102
    determining method of,
        102–103
defense mechanisms of buyer, 10
Della Femina, Jerry, 39–40
demonstrations, 119
desperation, 146–147
DiMaggio, Joe, 32
directness, 115
Disney, Walt, 135
Donald Type, 63–79
dramatic opening, 119
Dream Big (Shaw), 146
dress, 43, 82
Dunstan, Allen, 53

Durkin, Dorothy, 138
Dyer, Wayne, 14

Edison, Thomas, 28, 166
80/20 rule, 31, 147–148
Einstein, Albert, 64–65, 161
Einstein Type, 64–79
Eldar, Lue Ann, 42
Ellenthal, Ira, 60
empathy, 133–134
eulogy, 23
eye-movement test, 50–51

family tree exercise, 65, 66
fear
    cold calls and, 146–147
    insecurity and, 60
female bonding, 55
female buyers, 54–56
female salespeople, 170–171
femininity, 170–171
feng shui, 18–19
Field, Marshall, 57
financial responsibility, 167
focus, 28–30
follow-through, 167
Forbes, B. C., 17
Forte, Carolyn, 13
Frost, Robert, 83

Galileo, 28
gatekeepers, 140, 147–148
Gschwandtner, Gerhard, 21, 88
gifts, 44
goals
    in cold calling, 147–149
    planning daily and weekly, 25,
        30, 153
Gore, Al, 61
go signal, 115
Gray, John, 54–55
group presentations, 120

Guarascio, Phil, 55

Harper, Gena, 147
health, 160–163, 167
helping approach, 9–11
Hinton, Amanda, 132
homework, 13, 109–110, 117–118
homophobia, 40–41
honesty, 115

iconic types, 62–80
    adjusting to opposite style,
        75–76
    combinations of, 72
    described, 62–65
    difficulty relating to, 76–78
    family tree exercise, 65, 66
    identity charades exercise, 70
    learning from discomfort,
        78–79
    meeting yourself, 73–75
    personality role-playing,
        79–80
    recommendations and, 112
    seating chart exercise, 65–70
identity charades exercise, 70
improvising, 135–137
initial benefit statement (IBI), 110
inquiry process, 87–107
insecurity, importance of, 60
inspirational props, 30
integrity, 162

James, William, 147
Jefferson, Thomas, 63

Kennedy, John F., 19
kinesthetic processing, 47–50,
    51–52
Kirshbaum, Laurence J., 51
Klapish, Geoff, 89
Korda, Michael, 8

Lazarus, Shelly, 170
leading questions, 89–94,
    103–104
length of service, 13–14
Levenson, Sam, 168
listening, 41–42, 53, 133–134,
    135
luck, 17

Mackay, Harvey, 69
male bonding, 55
male buyers, 54–56
McAniff, Nora, 171–172
McCarron, William J., 43
McGowan, John, 57
meditation, 21–26
*Men Are From Mars, Women Are
    From Venus* (Gray), 54–55
Millet, Kate, 54
mirroring, 44–46
mission, 19–27
    mission statement, 20–26
    relaxation techniques and,
        21–26
    visualization techniques and,
        21–27
mission statement, 20–26
    business, 20–21, 23–24
    evaluating progress in, 25–26
    personal, 23
mood toys, 18–19
Moody, Roy B., 41
Murr, W. H., 27

naming names, 14
needs of client
    budget determination, 101
    converting to problems with
        solutions, 97–101
    establishing, 90, 95–97
    responding to, 110–113, 118
negative beliefs, 18

networking, 168–169
neuro-linguistic types, 46–52
    auditory, 47–51
    kinesthetic, 47–50, 51–52
    visual, 46, 47–51
Nicklaus, Jack, 26
Niebuhr, Reinhold, 16
nonverbal communication, 56–57
Norman, Greg, 81–82

objections, responding to, 130–133
observing, 42–44
office environment, observing, 43
1 percent solution, 153
open-ended questions, 56
Oprah Type, 62–79

paradigm shift, 34
persistence, 165–166
personality role-playing exercise,
    79–80
personal mission statement, 23
perspective-taking, 32–36
Petite, Jean Paul, 18
positive attitude, 15–19, 120,
    152–155
Powers, Wayne, 163
preemptive approach, 129–133
presentation, 109–121
    body of, 110–113
    caution signal, 115–116
    focus on close, 120
    go signal, 115
    to groups, 120
    initial benefit statement, 110
    needs of client in, 110–113, 118
    preparing for, 109–110,
        117–118
    prepresentation review,
        109–110
    price in, 116
    response versus, 110–113

stop signal, 114–115
taking prospect's temperature
    during, 113
tips for, 117–120
price discussions, 91, 94, 101, 116,
    131–133
prioritization, 30–31
problem-solving
    providing solutions, 97–101,
        134–137
    relaxation/visualization tech-
        niques for, 24–25
professionalism, 27–28, 31–32,
    161–162
prospecting, 139–144
    getting appointments, 143, 151
    getting through screens, 140,
        147–148
    identifying best prospects, 142
    organizing for, 141–142, 151,
        166
    preparing for, 139–140
    "sniffer" in, 142–143
    sources of prospects, 153
    success in, 156
    see also cold calls

questions
    background, 13–14, 88–89
    benefits, 105–106
    leading, 89–94, 103–104
    need questions, 90, 95–97
    open-ended, 56
    responding to, 89–94

recommendations, 112
referrals
    asking for, 126, 155
    using names of, 143, 155–156
Rehs, Howard L., 110
relating, 39–42
    relationships versus, 80–81

Relaxation Response, The
    (Benson), 21
relaxation techniques, 21–26
relaxed presentation style, 118
responsibility
    response-ability and, 32–36
    toward others, 8–14
    toward self, 14–32
rituals, 18–19
Robbins, Tony, 16, 160
Roker, Al, 62–63
Roosevelt, Eleanor, 152
Rose, Pete, 32
Ross, Steve, 30
Rubenstein, Howard J., 47
Rule of Three, 97–98

sales goals, 31
Sartre, Jean Paul, 17
screeners, 140, 147–148
seating chart exercise, 65–70
Seid, Lynne, 80
self-affirmation, 17
self-congratulation, 125–126
self-hypnosis techniques, 20–21
Seneca, 19
sex
    of buyer, 54–56
    dealing with opposite, 55–56
    of salesperson, 170–171
Shaw, Deborah Rosado, 146
Shaw, George Bernard, 31
Silva Mind Control, 20–21
smiling, 152
Smith, Jim, 144
Sobczak, Art, 95
soft inquiries, 13–14, 88–89
solutions, providing, 97–101,
    134–137

standing up, 152
statement of purpose, 20–21
stop signal, 114–115
support system, 168
surprise attacks, 133–135

Tartarella, Ron, 162
telephone calls
    attitude for, 152–155
    database management systems
      and, 141–142, 151, 166
    preparing for difficult, 24–25
    see also cold calls
10-10-10 system, 149, 151
Thoreau, Henry David, 20
Timeless Mind/Ageless Body
    (Chopra), 20–21
timing
    of close, 121
    of cold calls, 149
Tracy, Brian, 157
Trump, Donald J., 11, 63–64
trust, 52–54
Turner, Ted, 18

values, 55
visualization techniques, 21–27
    focus and, 29, 152
    problem-solving and, 24–25
visual processing, 46, 47–51
voice mail, 151

"warm" people, 60–61
Welch, Jack, 64
Winfrey, Oprah, 62
Woods, Tiger, 26

Yeats, William Butler, 33
"yes" trap, 137

about the authors

Carol Super has forged a career as one of the stellar sales producers in the country, even being singled out by her company for the honor of Salesperson of the Decade in recognition of her outstanding, record-setting sales performance. She works with such media giants as *Time, Newsweek, U.S. News & World Report, Sports Illustrated,* and *Business Week,* among others. As a trainer, she has designed and developed sales programs for a wide variety of sales teams and situations. As an innovator, she has introduced and implemented new sales and advertising approaches that have yielded extraordinary results for her clients. Ms. Super got her start in sales in the broadcast and communications arena, and also had a stint as a teacher, from which she gained experience and discipline which she puts to good use in her sales career. She holds an M.A. from Columbia University and her B.A. from Tulane University. She can be contacted at www.carolsuper.com or carolsuper@mindspring.com.

Ron David Gold is the Partner/Creative Director of MGMGold Communications, Ltd., a full-service Manhattan advertising agency. He is an award-winning copywriter/brander who developed the introductory marketing and advertising for Haagen Dazs and Alpine Lace, among many others. He is also a musician, photographer, and 3-D aficionado.